The Making of Modern Switzerland, 1848–1998

New Perspectives in German Studies

General Editors: Professor Michael Butler, Head of Department of German Studies, University of Birmingham and Professor William Paterson, Director of the Institute of German Studies, University of Birmingham

Over the last twenty years the concept of German studies has undergone major transformation. The traditional mixture of language and literary studies, related very closely to the discipline as practised in German universities, has expanded to embrace history, politics, economics and cultural studies. The conventional boundaries between all these disciplines have become increasingly blurred, a process which has been accelerated markedly since German unification in 1989/90.

New Perspectives in German Studies, developed in conjunction with the Institute for German Studies at the University of Birmingham, has been designed to respond precisely to this trend of the interdisciplinary approach to the study of German and to cater for the growing interest in Germany in the context of European integration. The books in this series will focus on the modern period, from 1750 to the present day.

Titles include:

Michael Butler, Malcolm Pender and Joy Charnley (*editors*)
THE MAKING OF MODERN SWITZERLAND 1848–1998

Jonathan Grix
THE ROLE OF THE MASSES IN THE COLLAPSE OF THE GDR

New Perspectives in German Studies
Series Standing Order ISBN 0–333–92430–4
(*outside North America only*)

You can receive future titles in this series as they are published by placing a standing order. Please contact your bookseller or, in case of difficulty, write to us at the address below with your name and address, the title of the series and the ISBN quoted above.

Customer Services Department, Macmillan Distribution Ltd, Houndmills, Basingstoke, Hampshire RG21 6XS, England

The Making of Modern Switzerland, 1848–1998

Edited by

Michael Butler
Professor of Modern German Literature
University of Birmingham

Malcolm Pender
Professor of German Studies
University of Strathclyde

and

Joy Charnley
Lecturer in French
University of Strathclyde

First published in Great Britain 2000 by
MACMILLAN PRESS LTD
Houndmills, Basingstoke, Hampshire RG21 6XS and London
Companies and representatives throughout the world

A catalogue record for this book is available from the British Library.

ISBN 0–333–80083–4

First published in the United States of America 2000 by
ST. MARTIN'S PRESS, LLC,
Scholarly and Reference Division,
175 Fifth Avenue, New York, N.Y. 10010

ISBN 0–312–23459–7

Library of Congress Cataloging-in-Publication Data
The making of modern Switzerland, 1848–1998 / edited by Michael Butler,
Malcolm Pender, and Joy Charnley.
p.   cm.
Includes bibliographical references and index.
ISBN 0–312–23459–7
1. Switzerland—Politics and government—1848—Congresses. 2. Political
ethics—Switzerland—Congresses. 3. European Union—Switzerland—Congresses.
I. Butler, Michael. II. Pender, Malcolm. III. Charnley, Joy, 1960–

DQ69 .M35   2000
949.407—dc21

00–027824

This book is printed on paper suitable for recycling and made from fully managed and sustained
forest sources.

10   9   8   7   6   5   4   3   2   1
09   08   07   06   05   04   03   02   01   00

Printed and bound in Great Britain by
Antony Rowe Ltd, Chippenham, Wiltshire

Contents

v

Preface

The 1990s were to be a decade of significance and celebration in Switzerland. The year 1991 would mark the 700th anniversary of the origins of the Helvetic Confederation and 1998 would be the 150th anniversary of the Constitution created in 1848, the only political transformation successfully effected in Europe in that year and one which laid the democratic foundations of the modern state. It was therefore ironic that events turned each of these occasions for celebration into deeply uncomfortable exercises in introspection and in reckoning with the past.

The 1991 anniversary was effectively ruined by the chance discovery in 1989 that the state had been keeping for many years secret files on some 900000 Swiss citizens, one-sixth of the adult population. In February of the same year Elisabeth Kopp, the first *Bundesrätin* in the country's history, was forced to resign in circumstances of scandal. In November the result of the referendum to abolish the Swiss army, in which over one-third of those voting supported the proposition, indicated radical alterations in attitudes. The damage done to Swiss self-perception was deep, and the malaise – in particular, the sense of having been betrayed in the so-called *Fichen-Affäre* – led writers, artists and intellectuals to organise a comprehensive boycott of the 1991 festivities.

The attempt to mark the defining moment of 1848 fell in its turn under a dark cloud. The release of secret documents under the 50-year rule in the USA, the general opening of archives after the collapse of the Soviet empire in 1989, and the increasing pressure from groups representing Holocaust survivors were factors that contributed to pressure for a thorough revision of Switzerland's role in the Second World War. In 1995 President Villiger made a formal admission of Swiss guilt in relation to her wartime refugee policy, but a year later the part played by Switzerland's leading banks in the laundering of gold looted by the Nazis from their conquered territories received massive coverage, above all in the United States. The image of Switzerland was further blackened. In 1997 President Koller pledged Swiss determination to make retribution for its past faults, and in

1998 the banks, under threat of sanctions in America, reached a settlement. Thus the anniversary year of 1998 was preceded by a crisis of identity in Switzerland which at its height was seen by the Swiss press as the worst period the country had passed through since the Second World War.

In the light of these events the sober and self-reflective note of much of the discussion on the foundation of modern Switzerland and on the significance of her unique institutions and federal structure is understandable. Additionally, however, this discussion acquires a dimension of urgency in view of the rapidly changing scene in Europe after the end of the Cold War. The fast-evolving political momentum of the European Union, its enlargement to include countries from Eastern Europe, and the establishment of the single currency pose huge dilemmas for Switzerland. How can she relate to a changing Europe without jettisoning the historic principle of neutrality which has served this small country so well and without losing her distinctive political and linguistic composition?

The chapters in this volume represent the record of two conferences held in Birmingham and Canterbury on 10 and 17 October 1998, respectively. Part I contains chapters based on papers dealing with historical and literary aspects of 1848 given in Birmingham and jointly organised by the Department of German Studies, University of Birmingham, and the Centre for Swiss Cultural Studies, University of Strathclyde. Part II includes chapters based on papers dealing with political and economic aspects of 1848 given at the University of Kent at Canterbury. Together, the two conferences provided a forum in the United Kingdom for the continuing debate within the Confederation, a debate whose rigour underlines the vitality of contemporary Switzerland, despite the difficulties she has faced and is still facing. It is to the credit of this small country that it is now firmly confronting its recent past and that it is able to see its long history of multicultural tolerance and democratic diversity in a fresh light. Indeed, the Swiss democratic model, established in 1848 and revised in 1874, together with the modernisation agreed by referendum in 1999, may well have concrete lessons to offer the countries of Europe as they seek to find viable ways of co-operation and integration. The 1990s may have been difficult years for the Confederation, but the chapters which follow show that this unique country possesses the imagination and energy to deal successfully with the problems which lie ahead and to contribute fresh impulses to the general European debate on national identities and cultures which will undoubtedly inform the early years of the new millennium.

The editors wish to record here their gratitude to the Swiss Embassy in London, especially to René Schaetti, Thomas Gürber and Wolfgang Brülhart, for their encouragement and support, and to the Stiftung Pro Helvetia both for financial support of the two conferences and for a subvention towards the publication costs of this volume.

MICHAEL BUTLER
JOY CHARNLEY
MALCOLM PENDER

Notes on the Contributors

Urs Bugmann studied German literature, literary theory, and journalism at Zurich University. He has worked as a publisher's reader, editor-in-chief of a bookmarket magazine and as cultural editor of a daily newspaper. He is now responsible for literature and theatre on the *Luzerner Neueste Nachrichten*. His publications include *Bewältigungsversuch. Thomas Bernhards autobiographische Schriften* (1981) and 'Vom Kleinmachen unter hohem Horizont' in *Literatur in der Schweiz. Text + Kritik* (1998).

Rémy Charbon studied German language and literature, modern and contemporary history and European folk literature in Zurich and Berlin. He currently teaches modern German literature at the universities of Fribourg (Switzerland) and Geneva. His main research interests are in Swiss literature from the eighteenth century to the present day, the literature of the German Democratic Republic and the relationship between history and literature. His most recent book is a study of the influence of literature on politics in Switzerland from 1798 to 1848, *O Schweizerland, du schöne Braut* (1998).

Clive H. Church holds a Jean Monnet Chair of European Studies at the University of Kent (Canterbury). He works on political and theoretical aspects of European integration and on Switzerland. He has written widely on Swiss domestic politics and the country's relationship with Europe. Among his books are *Revolution and Red Tale* (1981), and edited volumes, *Aspects of Switzerland: Sources and Reflections* (1986) and *Approaching the Channel Tunnel* (1987). A jointly edited commentary, *The Penguin Guide to EU Treaties* and a textbook on Swiss politics and government are due to appear shortly.

Thomas Cottier is Professor of International Law at the University of Berne and adviser to the Swiss government on the GATT negotiations. He is the Joint Editor of the definitive *Der Beitritt der Schweiz zur Europäischen Union. Brennpunkt und Auswirkungen* (1998).

Dominik Furgler is Economic Counsellor and Head of the Economic Department of the Swiss Embassy, London. He studied law in Fribourg (Switzerland). After completing his doctorate in private international law and working for the Union Bank of Switzerland, he joined the Swiss Diplomatic Service in 1985, working for the Financial and Economic Division until 1990 and the Swiss Delegation at the OECD in Paris until 1993. From 1993 to 1997 he was Head of Information and Press Officer of the Swiss (European) Integration Office.

Wolf Linder is Professor of Politics and Director of the Institute for Swiss Politics at the University of Berne. His research interests lie in the field of democratic theory and processes. He is an adviser to the Swiss government, especially on the differences between language communities and their responses to referenda. His latest book is *Schweizerische Demokratie* (1999).

Thomas Maissen is a historical analyst with the *Neue Zürcher Zeitung* and completing his *Habilitation* on early modern republicanism in Zurich and the Swiss Confederation. His research interests lie in the history of political ideas, cultural identity and Swiss history. His recent publications include (with Kate Burri) *Bilder aus der Schweiz, 1939–1945* (1997), *Vom Sonderbund zum Bundesstaat* (1998) and 'Fighting for Faith? The Experience of the Sonderbund Campaign', in Joy Charnley and Malcolm Pender (eds), *Switzerland and War* (1999).

Andrew Williams is Reader in International Relations at the University of Kent (Canterbury). He studied at the University of Keele and the Institut de Hautes Etudes Internationales in Geneva. He worked for a number of years for the Centre for the Applied Study of International Negotiation, particularly on a Ford Foundation project on East–West *rapprochement*. His main research interests are in international organisation, international conflict resolution and international history. Recent publications include *Failed Imagination? New World Orders of the Twentieth Century* (1998).

The Editors

Michael Butler is Professor of Modern German Literature at the University of Birmingham. His main research interests lie in post-1945

German and German-Swiss literature, and the literature of the German Democratic Republic. His books include *The Novels of Max Frisch* (1976), *The Plays of Max Frisch* (1984), *Frisch: 'Andorra'* (1985, 1994) (edited with Malcolm Pender), *Rejection and Emancipation: Writing in German-Speaking Switzerland 1945–1991* (1991) and (ed.), *The Narrative Fiction of Heinrich Böll: Social Conscience and Literary Achievement* (1994).

Joy Charnley is Lecturer in French at the University of Strathclyde (Glasgow). She is currently working on seventeenth-century travel-writing and women writers in the *Suisse romande*. Her recent publications include *Pierre Bayle: Reader of Travel Literature* (1998) and (as editor) *25 Years Emancipation? Women in Switzerland 1971–1996* (1998). She is co-editor of a new series, Occasional Papers in Swiss Studies (published under the aegis of the Centre for Swiss Cultural Studies at Strathclyde).

Malcolm Pender is Professor of German Studies in the University of Strathclyde (Glasgow). His main research interests are in post-1945 German literature, especially the literature of German-speaking Switzerland on which he has published widely. His books include *Max Frisch: His Work and its Swiss Background* (1979), *The Creative Imagination and Society: Aspects of the Swiss 'Künstlerroman' in the Twentieth Century* (1985), *Max Frisch: 'Biedermann und die Brandstifter'* (1988) and *Contemporary Images of Death and Sickness: a Theme in German-Swiss Literature* (1998). He is also co-editor of Occasional Papers in Swiss Studies (Strathclyde).

Part I

1
The 1848 Conflicts and their Significance in Swiss Historiography

Thomas Maissen

What does it take to make a revolution successful? How was it possible that, of all the countries concerned, Switzerland was the only one to see the success of its liberal and national movement in 1848? It was a success in a double sense: firstly, there was no political reaction and repression as elsewhere, the achievements of 1848 were not seriously threatened either by foreign powers or by internal opponents; and secondly, it was a lasting success, for from 1848 until today there has been constitutional and institutional continuity, making it possible to celebrate the 150th anniversary of modern Switzerland. Such continuity, which in addition has been peaceful, might not much impress a British audience that traces its national roots as far back as 1066, 1215 or even 1689 and 1707. But one has to compare modern Switzerland to the fate of the other continental countries: none of them has been spared territorial modifications or institutional and constitutional struggles throughout the last 150 years, and most have suffered enormously from these changes. Only the small Alpine republic has somehow muddled through the era of the nation state without too much harm. It has become more obvious over the last few years, however, that this success story has its dark spots, too, and it is high time for the Swiss to say goodbye to an unrealistically heroic view of their past. Nevertheless, they can be grateful for what happened in the 1840s, for a 'very civil war', as Joachim Remak has ambiguously called it,[1] ended a lasting period of internal strife and insecurity and led to an institutional reconstruction of the old Confederation. Another outcome of that crisis was always possible: Switzerland could have broken apart in 1847 or the confrontation could have ended with a stalemate, leaving the federal state with its archaic structure. It is not the historian's job to discuss the 'what if' question, but it is not difficult to imagine what it could have meant to a traditional Switzerland of 22 sovereign, but tiny cantons to be confronted with the building of nations in the second half of the nineteenth century, especially the Italian *Risorgimento* and the German *Reichsgründung*.

The conflicts leading to the new state of 1848

To understand how close the decision of 1848 really was, we have to look first at the preceding critical years.[2] The Swiss *ancien régime* fell in 1798, under simultaneous pressure from Napoleon's revolutionary troops and the claim for full citizenship and political participation widely diffused among subjects in the countryside and in the *Gemeine Herrschaften*, the areas dominated by several cantons conjointly. The product of this upheaval was the Helvetische Republik, a centralised state in line with the modern French rational model, which did not last. In 1803 Napoleon imposed a new constitution that again respected the rights of the sovereign cantons. Through the treaties of Vienna and Paris in 1815, Switzerland was granted eternal neutrality, and through the *Bundesvertrag* it again became the union of almost independent states it had been until 1798. The only national institution was the Diet (Tagsatzung), a congress of cantonal envoys who voted according to their government's instructions when they met in the *Vorort*, the capital which alternated every two years between Zurich, Berne and Lucerne. There was no centralised administration, and the competence of the Tagsatzung was limited to foreign and security policy. Thus it was quite deliberately that the name *Bundesvertrag* was chosen in 1815: this was no constitution among citizens, but a pact between confederate states. Yet it was this *Bundesvertrag* which contained the legal nucleus of the later conflicts. In paragraph 6, we read that the cantons were not to have separate alliances among each other which might be detrimental to the Confederation or to other cantons (keine dem allgemeinen Bund oder den Rechten anderer Kantone nachtheilige Verbindungen). On the other hand, according to paragraph 4, each canton was entitled to ask other cantons for help if it was in danger. Finally, paragraph 12 contained a guarantee for the monasteries and their property. The *Bundesvertrag* was barely contested until 1830 when once again, a French revolution brought about changes in many other European countries too. Already before Louis-Philippe's triumph in late summer, the Ticino had adopted a new, liberal constitution. Ten other cantons followed, yielding to the pressure of popular meetings in autumn and winter 1830; this was the case in Zurich, Berne, Lucerne, Solothurn, Fribourg, Schaffhausen, St Gallen, Aargau, Thurgau and Vaud. Here, modern liberal structures were founded: people's sovereignty within a representative democracy, separation of powers, personal and economic freedom. As there was political unrest in other cantons too, there were soon two opposing blocks within the Confederation which even formed alliances for some time: the conservative group (Sarner Bund) consisted of the founding cantons of Uri, Schwyz and Unterwalden, with Zug, Basle, Neuchâtel and the Valais, whereas the liberal Siebnerkonkordat brought together Zurich, Berne, Lucerne, Solothurn, St Gallen, Aargau and Thurgau. The strong opposition of traditional thinking, which was manifest also in liberal cantons, made the revision of the 1815 *Bundesvertrag* impossible although a new constitution, the so-called *Bundesurkunde*, was proposed in 1832/3. Yet the revision failed not only because of the conservatives but also because on the other side the so-called radicals argued that the *Bundesurkunde* would not go far enough.

Thus, from 1833 onwards, we have three major political groups struggling for power within the cantons. We have to keep in mind that these were not the political parties we know nowadays but loose associations of men who shared political ideas. The differences between them were often subject to change and owed much to the particular situation in each canton and to other circumstances. Thus we must not be surprised that there are several famous cases of 'apostasy', liberals of the 1830s who changed their ideas and became leading members of the conservative group. The most famous was the future leader of the Sonderbund, Constantin Siegwart-Müller. Bearing in mind the fluidity of the political boundaries, let us have a closer look at the three groups.[3]

Liberals: The Swiss liberal tradition was strongly influenced by Benjamin Constant's thinking insofar as it defended the goals of the French Revolution but, horrified by the *Terreur*, insisted firmly on the institutional means of avoiding its mistakes. For Constant, personal freedom and property went hand in hand; they allowed an individualistic elite to handle the commonwealth while the state did not intervene in their private affairs. The people was sovereign, but its representatives were almost fully independent of its will; as for the representatives, they were controlled by a constitution which could not be modified easily. Thus, the people's sovereignty found its expression and at the same time its limits in voting a constitution and electing the parliament, rights which were often restricted by census. Many liberals even went so far as to consider the parliament itself sovereign, once it had been elected on a constitutional basis; often, they considered the British parliament as their model. Still, it was the liberal intention to enlarge popular participation: in a fairly optimistic view of human beings, education was supposed to form good and skilful citizens who could acquire property, thus learn responsibility and fully participate in political power.

Radicals: Radicalism differed from liberalism mainly in its interpretation of people's sovereignty, whose exercise was seen as much less formal and clearly limiting the arbitrariness of its representatives. The radical tradition goes back to the Anglo-Saxon roots of John Wilkes who called for universal suffrage and also to Thomas Paine and Jeremy Bentham's egalitarian utilitarianism. But in Switzerland, the influence of Rousseau, of the French Jacobins and of German refugees, namely Ludwig Snell, was more important, as was the memory of the Swiss unitarian movement after 1798 and some Swiss political thinkers, Ignaz Paul Vital Troxler being the most important and most interesting. The unitarian theories produced centralised governments in some cantons, especially Vaud, and also claimed a strong central power for the whole nation. Such a government should also intervene, according to the radicals, in economic and social affairs, which liberals wished to keep free from interference from the state. The main distinction concerned sovereignty and the role of constitution and revolution. For liberals, a revolution was legitimate when it led to a constitution based on sovereignty of the people; but once a constitution was established, further evolution had to proceed within its settled rules. As the liberal *Neue Zürcher Zeitung* put it in 1846, the Constitution must restrain the people from becoming an absolutist ruler.[4] On the other hand, Henri Druey, a radical leader and later member of the first national government, the

Bundesrat, stated in Rousseauian terms, that the supreme will of the people must not be bound by the Constitution which is a product of that will and not a contract.[5] Thus the radicals could proclaim the people's right to revolution (*Volksrecht auf Revolution*)[6] which was one of the dynamic elements in the crisis leading to the Sonderbund War.

Conservatives: The other dynamic element was situated, even if it sounds paradoxical, in the conservative camp. To understand this, we must differentiate further the varying components of that camp. What united them was their hostility towards the modernist elements which we find among radicals as well as among liberals: anticlericalism, secular education, rationalism, positivism, materialism, belief in progress. To all that, the conservatives opposed revelation and religious faith, the legacy of history and tradition, prescriptive law, old privileges and alliances, an organic view of the state and the Church linked to a metaphysical order. These convictions were shared by Catholic as well as by Protestant conservatives; the latter ruled in Basle, Neuchâtel and until 1846, Geneva, and always formed an influential opposition in the biggest liberal cantons of Zurich, Berne and Vaud. Yet the Protestant conservatives were eclipsed by the dynamics of the 1840s caused by their Catholic counterparts. Here again we have to distinguish between the traditionalist particularists or (in the German sense of the word) 'federalists' on the one hand and the 'ultras' on the other. The particularists stuck to the century-old cantonal sovereignty and the solemn role of the Church in everyday life; they often belonged to the traditional patrician elites of the *ancien régime* and were, in the strict sense of the word, conservative insofar as they did not see why the *Bundesvertrag* of 1815 should be modified. Unlike the particularists, the 'ultras' thought that the struggle against liberal modernity must be fought with modern weapons: they relied on popular religious feelings, but also on the sovereignty of the people. Thus they fought the restricted circles of the ruling liberal elites, changed the Constitution with the help of popular movements, and introduced democratic instruments, especially the so-called 'veto', a predecessor of the referendum. The most famous leaders of the 'ultras' were the farmer Joseph Leu von Ebersol and the aforementioned Lucerne Schultheiss, the Mayor Constantin Siegwart-Müller. The latter was to be the 'spiritus rector' of the Sonderbund, and he even went so far as to develop a plan for changing the boundaries and governments in other Swiss cantons after a possible victory in a war. Such a revolutionary outcome would have guaranteed a stable equilibrium between Catholics and Protestants, between liberals and conservatives; it could never have been imagined by the traditionalist particularists who were so fond of the ancient laws which they wished to perpetuate among confederates.

Having sketched in these details about the main political groups, the early Socialist movement being of little importance in the Swiss context of 1848, we can now give a brief overview of the *confessional* dynamics of the 1840s that led to the Sonderbund War. We must recall that among the regenerated cantons of 1830 were Lucerne, Solothurn, Fribourg and the Ticino, all wholly Catholic, to whom we may add St Gallen and Aargau which both had a large Catholic population. With Protestant cantons like Basle, Neuchâtel and Geneva in the conservative camp, it was obvious to all contemporaries that there was a political, not a religious confrontation on a national level, which during the 1830s remained unsettled. Yet, within the cantons, confrontations soon intensified over the closely connected issues of the Church and education. As early as 1834, seven liberal cantons tried to establish a Catholic national archbishopric under state control, but protests mainly in the Bernese Jura and diplomatic interventions by the Pope and France put a stop to that initiative. In 1839, the liberal government of Zurich appointed the rationalist theologian David Friedrich Strauss to its recently founded university; popular unrest, mainly in the countryside, opposed this *Religionsgefahr*, the threat to the Zwinglian orthodoxy. The government yielded and in the coup of September 1839 the conservatives took power. Throughout the country the impact was enormous: the conservatives adopted the techniques of popular assemblies and riots and Zurich, one of the three *Vororte*, highly industrialised and a flagship of the liberal movement, changed camps. What followed was a series of coups: the liberals won in the Ticino and they resisted conservative Catholic insurrections in Aargau and Solothurn. But after a first victory in 1839, they lost the Valais in 1844 following heavy casualties, whereas in Lucerne, another *Vorort*, a popular movement under the leadership of Joseph Leu von Ebersol ended in 1841 by peacefully establishing a conservative government.

Thus, around 1840 most cantons were touched by internal political unrest. The reaction of one of them, Aargau, raised the problem to a national level. In early 1841, after the aforementioned insurrection, the radical government closed down the monasteries which were considered to be the nucleus of the armed revolt and this in spite of the fact that, as mentioned, the rights of the monasteries had been explicitly guaranteed in the 1815 *Bundesvertrag*.

The Catholic cantons subsequently protested against this illegal act on the part of the Argovian government, but the liberal majority of the Tagsatzung declared in 1843 that it was satisfied with the reconstitution of the four Argovian nunneries. Even among conservative Protestants, notably in Zurich, few were prepared to defend the rights of the monks who since Zwingli had constantly been on the receiving end of criticism from the reformed Church. The conservative case became even more difficult among Protestants in 1844 when Lucerne appointed Jesuits to run its seminary. This symbol of the Counter-Reformation met with the traditional hatred of the Protestants and of many enlightened Catholics too. Here we can best see the difference between the conservative 'particularists' and the 'ultras': the cautious traditionalists opposed the appointment because they did not want to provoke religious unrest but the 'ultras' imposed it, as it enabled them to mobilise the flock of believers against radical aggression. Thus the confrontation became fiercer and fiercer as the extremes in both camps, 'ultras' and radicals, took over. In December 1844 a first armed attempt to overthrow the Lucerne government failed miserably. A second *Freischarenzug* with radical volunteers not only from Lucerne, but also from many surrounding cantons, was heavily defeated on 1 April 1845 when over 100 men lost their lives. As it was obvious that the liberal cantons had not prevented the attack from their territory and had even let the volunteers arm themselves in their arsenals, the scandal was tremendous at the Tagsatzung. The fury of the Catholic conservatives grew even further in the summer of 1845 when Robert Steiger, a Lucernese radical leader of the second *Freischarenzug*, who had been sentenced to death, managed to escape from prison and was welcomed as a hero in the liberal cantons. A month later, a former guerrilla assassinated Joseph Leu von Ebersol while he was asleep.

Thus, in 1845, there was little space left between those who wanted to fight the radical aggression against Christianity and law and those who thought they were opposing the ultramontane reaction against modernity and individual rights. The once large *juste milieu* that ran from moderate conservatism to moderate liberalism, had to choose. It was not by chance that immediately after the second *Freischarenzug*, the liberal Jonas Furrer was elected burgomaster of Zurich – the conservative regime, considered a tool of the Jesuits, was abolished. Similarly, in Vaud the liberal government was overthrown by a radical revolution because the population did not agree with its moderate position towards the Jesuits. As a result of the second *Freischarenzug* and the ambivalent role of the Bernese government, the radicals gained power in that canton, too: Ulrich Ochsenbein, a leader of the volunteers, became a member and later Schultheiss, mayor of the government. In that role, at the head of a *Vorort*, he was to become president of the Tagsatzung in 1847.

At this point, we have to look at the *institutional* conflict. Since the failed revision of 1832/3, Switzerland had been split between the particularist federalists and the partisans of a strong, modern nation state. Often enough, the obvious lack of efficiency of the Tagsatzung had been the subject of complaint; often enough, pressure from surrounding monarchies like France and Austria had shown that the Confederation could not match the power of centralised states. In addition, since 1839 the Tagsatzung had been watching the series of coups without intervening to settle them; on the contrary, Lucerne as a *Vorort* in 1844 played a major part in worsening the crisis in the Valais. But it was not enough that Switzerland lacked an executive that could impose law and order; there was not even a legal procedure in sight which could furnish it. The 1815 *Bundesvertrag* did not contain a single paragraph about its revision, as it was meant to be eternal. Already in 1832/3 the conservative cantons declared that they considered the Confederation a pact between independent cantons that could only be revised if all of them agreed. How could things continue as they were in the mid-1840s, once feelings among confederates had become much more bitter than they were a dozen years earlier?

What became the final step towards disunion paradoxically ended up resolving the constitutional and institutional problems. On 11 December 1845 Uri, Schwyz, Unterwalden, Lucerne, Zug, Fribourg and the Valais formed a defensive alliance, labelled the Sonderbund (separatist league) by its antagonists as soon as they found out about it. The seven cantons, all of them wholly Catholic, justified their alliance by referring to the guerrilla attacks which the Tagsatzung had not prevented. But this time, unlike the formally correct appointment of the Jesuits, the conservatives had chosen an illegal way themselves: the aforementioned paragraph 6 of the 1815 *Bundesvertrag* stated that separate alliances which might be detrimental to the Confederation or other cantons were forbidden. This danger could not be denied: the surrounding conservative monarchies, especially Guizot's France and Metternich's Austria, were interested in a weak and conservative Switzerland and did not hide their sympathy for the Sonderbund. The future of the Confederation was at stake: it was possible that the conservative cantons might form a separate union or change the existing one, as we have seen with Siegwart-Müller's project.

The new threat definitely clarified the situation. At the Tagsatzung of August 1846, only ten cantons voted for abolishing the Sonderbund. Five cantons were still neutral but after a short civil war, the radicals gained control of Geneva, and there was only one vote missing for a majority of 12 votes among the 22 cantons. The Catholic Appenzell-Innerrhoden would not furnish it, nor would Neuchâtel, which still had the King of Prussia as its sovereign. That left Basle, where a peaceful revision of the Constitution did not convulse the conservative government, or Fribourg, where the radicals attempted a coup in early 1847 in order to leave the Sonderbund, but were easily defeated. In the elections of May 1847 St Gallen decided for Switzerland. Until then, conservatives and liberals had had exactly the same number of seats in that canton, and thus St Gallen had not yet chosen its camp. Once a small, Catholic constituency unexpectedly voted liberal, there was a majority of two seats and St Gallen joined the majority at the Tagsatzung. This case shows how very close the decision was, not only in St Gallen, but all over Switzerland. It even seems that one small village in that constituency, Amden, was decisive for the whole country because, as a form of protest, the inhabitants voted against their own – conservative – magistrate.

This leads us, after the political, the confessional and the institutional, to the *economic* conflict, the fourth one leading up to 1848. The magistrate of that small village of Amden was accused, immediately before the vote, of having speculated on flour while the villagers were starving. Since 1845, Switzerland had been suffering from potato rot and famine, the same one that caused catastrophe in Ireland. The Swiss situation was not as disastrous, but it was difficult enough and contributed to radicalising the two camps which accused each other of worsening the situation. In this period of early industrialisation, there were also other reasons for existential insecurity and even violent protest: in 1832, the rural town of Uster near Zurich experienced a riot of weavers and domestic labourers who destroyed the newly installed mechanical looms and finally burnt down the whole factory. Thus, the manufacturers, who formed an important group among the new liberal elites, were soon confronted with serious unrest among the less privileged who in 1830, had helped them to get rid of the old patrician rulers. It was again no coincidence that the imprisoned rioters of 1832 were freed in 1839, after the conservative coup against the liberal regime – the country dwellers often combined religious and economic feelings against the new elites. Let us mention a final economic problem, the unification of a national market. Already the *Bundesurkunde* of 1832/3 had proposed a federal monopoly on customs, on the post, on coinage and measures, but this attempted revision failed and traditional particularism continued. Protectionism on the part of the cantons thus opposed the liberty to carry out a trade and they defended their own citizens and their products while being unable to defend common Swiss interests against the bigger surrounding powers. The Tagsatzung and non-governmental institutions, such as the Schweizerische Gewerbeverein, founded in 1843, tried to find solutions within the old system, but they did not agree about the procedures and failed. Among other effects, this meant a notable delay in railway-building. By 1848 a single line, from Strasbourg, had barely touched Swiss soil at Basle and the cities of Zurich and Baden had just been connected by about 20 kilometres of track. There were plenty of other initiatives, but they were as yet unable to overcome cantonal selfishness.

In connection with the economic problems we must look at *social* change due to industrialisation and the new, liberal public space. On one side of society, we have a growing group of dependent workers and petty peasants with very limited financial means – in these difficult times, many of them were ready for visions, be it the religious faith of the ancestors or the liberal prediction of eternal progress. Metternich himself judged the riots and the radical triumph in Geneva as the first successful Socialist revolution on the continent. But in the end, even the radicals in Switzerland turned out to be rather moderate and often even quite elitist. Rather than a social movement on the part of the lower classes, the Swiss regeneration involved changing those in power: the old urban patricians who were at the head of the cantons until 1830 yielded their place to the *bourgeois des talents*, the liberal professions, the civil servants, and the entrepreneurs who most often originated in the many municipalities to whom full civil rights were given only after 1798. This rapid and often radicalising exchange of elites can best be seen in Berne, which went from the old aristocrat Rudolf von Wattenwyl, mayor in 1830, to the moderate regime of the liberal Schnell family from the municipality of Burgdorf, who had to hand over power to the radical Charles Neuhaus in 1839; in his turn, after the catastrophe of the *Freischarenzüge*, Neuhaus yielded to the even more radical group surrounding the lawyers Ochsenbein and Jakob Stämpfli, born into a modest farming family only 26 years earlier. Thus the experience that the revolution maybe does not eat but overthrows its own children is endemic in these years in the usually tranquil Swiss cantons.

We have looked at the political, the religious, the institutional, the economic and the social aspects of this unrest which characterises the regeneration, especially during the years after 1839. Yet we must state that contemporaries mostly experienced the events leading to the new state of 1848 as a *political* crisis: one coup followed another, almost every canton had its successful and failed upheavals, and the Tagsatzung was for a long time unable to intervene and procure peace among the different factions. The longer it went on the more even moderate people agreed that there could only be Alexander's solution for the Gordian knot in Swiss policy. In the summer of 1847 finally, one group, the liberal one, had the power and the united force to impose solutions in the controversial matters: the 12 cantons decided to dissolve the Sonderbund, to expel the Jesuits and to revise the Constitution. The legal foundation for the last two decrees was thin: the Jesuit question belonged to the jurisdiction of the canton concerned and as mentioned, the 1815 *Bundesvertrag* did not provide for a revision through majority decision. The Sonderbund therefore opposed the edicts and mobilised under the leadership of Ulrich von Salis, a Protestant conservative. Ironically, another Protestant conservative, Guillaume Henri Dufour from Geneva, was named General of the Tagsatzung troops, which turned out to be the better choice: after a short campaign of about 20 days with roughly 100 casualties the Sonderbund surrendered.

The cases of Dufour and von Salis show once again that this was a political, rather than a religious conflict, and that the decisive political contest for the extremes was to convince the hesitating *juste milieu*. With their patriotic reference to the Swiss nation, the radicals succeeded far better. Besides the political conflict of course, the confessional animosities did a lot to mobilise the ordinary soldiers on both sides, but they were not at the origin of the war. What was at stake can best be seen in the words of two leading Lucerne politicians: the liberal Kasimir Pfyffer did not join the Sonderbund troops because, as he put it, 'every Swiss should first consider himself a confederate and only after that the citizen of a canton'.[7] On the other hand, the conservative Philipp Anton von Segesser wrote immediately after the lost war: 'To me, Switzerland is only of interest because Lucerne – which is my country (*Vaterland*) – lies in it. If this canton no longer exists as a free, sovereign part of the Confederation, I care as much for the latter as for Tartary.'[8] Modern nation state or traditional confederation, that was the question in 1847 and 1848. Of course, both sides called it a fight for freedom and democracy, but judged from today, we clearly see on both sides the shortcomings of this rhetoric. Out of fear of direct – and conservative – democracy, the victorious liberals abolished in Zug and Schwyz the Landsgemeinde and in Lucerne the 'veto', a kind of referendum. In addition, without the military threat from the neighbouring cantons and many legalistic tricks, the new radical regime in Fribourg would have given way much earlier than 1856.

Still, these problematic aspects were eclipsed by the success of the new Constitution, quickly designed in February and March 1848, discussed in the parliaments of the cantons and at the Tagsatzung, accepted in a referendum by a big majority of voters and 15 and a half cantons, and proclaimed on 12 September 1848. As it is impossible to go into too much detail here, I will just mention the most important aspects: a national executive, the federal council; a bicameral parliament according to the American system, thus guaranteeing considerable influence to the small cantons; several freedom rights, such as – to some extent – universal suffrage for men and freedom of settlement; unification of customs, post, coinage, measures and weights; further unification in military issues; federal competence to promote the commonwealth, through public enterprises or a national university. It is clear that even besides the obvious model of the USA, many foreign ideas influenced the Constitution of 1848. Yet, it was declared a 'home-grown' Swiss creation from the beginning to avoid the hated memory of the Helvetic Republic of 1798.

Let us now return to the initial question: what did it take to make the Swiss revolution of 1848 successful? Maybe first of all the fact that it was not a real revolution or at least managed fairly well to hide its revolutionary aspects. The Tagsatzung was the only national authority and it was the Tagsatzung that suppressed the rebellion of the Sonderbund; as the war was quickly won, there was no period of anarchy during which foreign powers could have intervened under some pretext. Once the military solution had been imposed, there remained no serious internal opposition either; Protestant and Catholic conservatives surrendered and accepted the new Constitution, and those who did not, did not resist openly but went on hoping for help from abroad. But that became impossible for several months after February 1848, when first France, then Austria, Prussia, and almost all German states had plenty to do themselves with their own domestic revolutions. The Tagsatzung used precisely this period without external threat for writing and voting the new Constitution that went much further than one would have expected in late 1847. Yet, the fathers of the Constitution could refer to the failed *Bundesurkunde* of 1832 and – maybe even more important – to almost 20 years of modern parliamentarianism and constitutionalism on a cantonal level. The revolution had actually been going on since 1830, and even though many of the fathers of modern Switzerland were surprisingly young, they all had considerable experience in handling political crisis. This led them finally to remain neutral and stay outside the European struggles of 1848 and 1849, although there was a great deal of pressure, even within the government itself, to join the liberal camp in the general 'fight for principles'. This decision, which maybe saved the country from a military intervention after the victory of reaction all over Europe, was taken according to the Swiss state's *raison d'état*; but it also reflected two essential differences from the revolutionary movements abroad. In 1847 and 1848, there was neither a *social* nor a *national* question in Switzerland. While France installed a new Napoleon to save the country from class war, the Swiss workers and peasants were still far from developing class-consciousness; their identity was confessional or political, cantonal or national, but barely social. On the other hand, a quite homogeneous, national *bourgeoisie des talents* was already formed and ready to take power and responsibilities, but also to co-opt new members from the lower classes to whom they suggested education as the means of social ascent. While social conflicts were still to come, the national frontiers had already been clarified for some time. In the critical years from 1798 to 1815, Switzerland had found its territorial form which was not seriously questioned afterwards; if the Swiss did not agree about the future institutions of their country, that did not mean that they wanted to split it up or join another state. Through newspapers, the army, clubs and societies, there had been, since 1815, an ever-extending national public domain. Characteristically, there were French- and German-speaking cantons in both camps of the Sonderbund War and the boundary between the moderate eastern liberals and the interventionist western radicals was not the famous *Röstigraben*, but somewhere between Berne and Zurich. Thus the Swiss Confederation somehow succeeded in bringing a pre-national, political, republican identity into the era of the democratic national state. It has lasted since then, thanks to integrating myths and thanks to a constitution which allows continuous adaptation to a world that is changing faster and faster.

Swiss historiography about the Sonderbund and the new Confederation

The second part of this essay deals with the aftermath of 1847 and 1848 in Swiss historiography. Of course, many contemporaries wrote their memoirs or impressions and thus forged the ideas of their successors.[9] The leader of the Sonderbund, Siegwart-Müller, published his account in 1866 and the title – 'The victory of violence over law' – says almost everything. It is an apologia for the Sonderbund which, as Siegwart admits, was by then often criticised even among those who were once its members. Siegwart goes on to proclaim that 'centralisation' is the 'murderer of people's freedom' and the separation of state and Church leads to the decline of virtue and Christendom.[10] Siegwart's former secretary, Joseph Balthasar Ulrich, also chooses a significant title in order to contradict liberal terminology. The Sonderbund War was known as a *Bundesexekution*, the execution of a federal decision against rebels, whereas Ulrich, who himself served in the war, entitles his book *Bürgerkrieg in der Schweiz*: a civil war against the acknowledged legal maxims and clear rules of the Confederation (anerkannte Rechtsgrundsätze und klare Bundesbestimmungen).

Balthasar, who finished his book in 1850, sees the tragedy of ancient, original, Catholic Switzerland as a prelude to the fight for principles in the whole of Europe, the revolutions as an effect of planned conspiracy. Yet he hopes that the new Confederacy in spite of its unitarian and factious character can be 'a rampart against injustice and arbitrariness, a rampart for the freedom of confessions and Christian life, a bond of reconciliation and union of the people and a bulwark for an independent country'.[11] Here we see the readiness of many of the vanquished to participate *faute de mieux* in the new state; even Bernhard Meyer, Siegwart's co-leader in the Sonderbund and later exiled in Munich, summons his partisans in summer 1848 to vote for the new Constitution, because a refusal would either continue the chaos of illegality or provoke a real unitarian constitution that would finally smash the rights of the cantons.[12]

The most interesting conservative voice is perhaps that of Gallus Jakob Baumgartner, an 'apostate' like Siegwart-Müller. In 1832, Baumgartner edited the liberal *Bundesurkunde*, but as a Catholic he switched camps around 1840. Consequently he is very critical of the radical 'tyranny' and the illegal measures that led to the new Constitution, but he welcomes the Constitution itself which could promote internal welfare and avoid disunion against foreign parts. Baumgartner is convinced that an evolution of the particularist Confederation was inevitable and cannot be revoked, but at the same time, he calls for republican virtues and simplicity to counterbalance the dangerous, corruptive influence of foreign courts and modern, mob-led politics.[13] In an accurate analysis of the new Constitution, Baumgartner states in 1851 that it gave the federal institutions the maximum power that Swiss tradition could admit; yet, the real danger was not centralisation but the fact that the ruling liberals illegally abused their powers, and that the big cantons, the winners of the war, flouted the national institutions they themselves installed while the losers lacked the strength for such a policy.[14]

Similar in some ways to Baumgartner, the moderate liberal Niklaus Friedrich von Tschudi, also from St Gallen, keeps his distance from the factious extremes in both camps: the radicals have been acting illegally, but the Sonderbund has willingly risked an intervention of foreign powers. Thus its dissolution has become inevitable and corresponds to the nation's needs, interests and laws.[15]

The winners, like the radical Jakob Amiet from Solothurn, celebrate a victory of the 'nation against foreign, non-Swiss, completely non-national elements', that is the aristocracy, Rome and the Jesuits. Like many losers, liberals consider Swiss events a prelude to the uprising of peoples all over Europe, but unlike their adversaries, they see this as a positive step towards universal progress.[16] The Argovian J. Martin Rudolf describes the struggle against fanaticism, superstition and intolerance which led the innocent Catholic people to fight a hopeless war against their confederates. To him, the Swiss troops of his time are no longer in the mercenary tradition of the *ancien régime*, but have rediscovered the roots of their heroic ancestors like Winkelried and the warriors of St Jakob.[17] This is the path the liberal and national interpretation of the critical years had already established earlier[18] and one which was to develop further in the nineteenth century: while the original cantons semi-consciously continue the decadence and dependence of the *ancien régime*,[19] the liberal fighters for freedom are the true heirs of William Tell and the original struggle for independence and democracy.

Another lasting feature that made the Swiss revolution acceptable to many hesitating members of the *juste milieu* like the Bernese aristocrat Anton von Tillier[20] was the fame of Guillaume Henri Dufour. With his memoirs, which he wanted to be published only after his death, the general himself contributed to his lasting image as a chivalrous, moderate and modest soldier who did his duty and yet overcame the bad feelings of his enemies.[21] Even today Dufour remains, along with Tell, Niklaus von Flüe, Henri Dunant and Henri Guisan, one of the most popular historical heroes of Switzerland; many roads bear his name, as does the Dufourspitze, the only mountain in the Alps to be named after a real person. Dufour somehow symbolises the historical necessity of the Sonderbund War and the subsequent foundation of the new Confederation: a conservative himself, he obeyed the call of the nation and through his clemency integrated the vanquished into the new state. Although in reality many Catholics had a long way to go before accepting the federal state, the memory of Dufour could help them.

After all, they had to adopt the view of their enemies, as liberal historiography was to dominate for almost a century. The German refugee

Peter Feddersen, who witnessed the crisis already in Basle where he was naturalised, finished in 1866 a *History of the Regeneration*, describing it as an independent republican movement, 'without any foreign interference', heading towards a new order which reflected the growing national consciousness. Even if – according to Feddersen – liberal postulates like legal equality, religious freedom, unified law or freedom of trade were not fully imposed against particularist opposition, the reborn, powerful Confederation could set about many new tasks and reached a level from where further natural development became easy.[22] The major syntheses of the following decade mostly follow the same interpretation: the liberal movement is natural, some overreactions from the radicals, like the *Freischarenzüge*, deplorable, but the real and stubbornly defended crimes are the appointment of the Jesuits and the creation of the Sonderbund. A truly harmonious national policy wins with Dufour in an inevitable war and frees Switzerland from internal unrest and external influence: the wise masterpiece of a new constitution, beyond particularism and unitarianism, moderate even towards the losers and in full harmony with the Swiss federalist tradition, becomes, together with neutrality during the 1848 revolutions, the basis for further peaceful and organic prosperity. We can read this version in Karl Dändliker's national history of 1887, leading us from the conservative tyranny in Lucerne to the Constitution which finally strengthens national feelings and national power.[23] Similarly, Johannes Dierauer, in his fundamental *History of the Swiss Confederation*, opposes (and thus justifies) the patriotism of the *Freischaren* to the 'formal order of state' that clearly objects to their deeds; the Sonderbund crisis is an 'inescapable natural force', and the new Confederacy turns out to be an equally natural result of the 'indigenous old historical tradition and an ever-growing internal stimulus'.[24] Numa Droz, a former federal councillor, praises in his popular description of the regeneration the 'warm rays of the confederate spirit' of 1848.[25] In 1902, Theodor Curti, like Droz a former journalist and politician, publishes a chapbook about his country in the nineteenth century, telling, without disdain for the conservatives, an elementary drama about the bold liberals fulfilling the 'dream of a whole generation'.[26] Max Huber, in the midst of the First World War, calls the Constitution the 'most fortunate and important act in Swiss history'.[27] The interpretation of 1848 as a somehow transcendental stroke of luck can be read in many later texts, too.[28]

The loser's voice is not completely missing, as we have for example Joseph Hürbin from Lucerne, who blames the leaders of the Sonderbund for its defeat while the people were prepared to sacrifice themselves.[29] But Hürbin, who in 1903 was still complaining about the unitarian elements of the 1848 Constitution, is an exception. The liberal interpretation prevails, even if or rather because it points out what a decisive break the years between 1798 and 1848 really were: continuity, not revolution is the motto. In 1891, the Swiss national state invents and celebrates for the first time the tradition of the 1291 oath on the Rütli;[30] it is symptomatic that in the same year, the first member of the Catholic conservative party joins the Federal Council. In these years when the coalition of the non-Socialist parties, that is the different liberal groups, the conservative losers of 1848 and the farmers is formed, early history definitely becomes the focus of Swiss identity while the conflicts leading to 1848 are eclipsed.[31] Thus in 1898, there is no national jubilee; only Berne celebrates the memory because it is linked to its election as federal capital.[32]

A sober approach is also typical of mere historians of the Constitution: Carl Hilty, in 1891, sees the work of 1848 as nothing but the implementation of the *Bundesurkunde* of 1832 and a first step towards the revised Constitution of 1874 which installed truly democratic instruments like the referendum.[33] Similarly, Eduard His points out the continuities in constitutional thought and the decisive role of the democratic movement leading to the revision of 1874.[34] Andreas Heusler, in 1920, does not go that far and speaks of the 'fundamental upheaval' of 1848, but still points out the many compromises in the new Constitution.[35]

In the first half of the twentieth century, the liberal interpretation acquires a new element. In the first edition of his *Swiss History*, published in 1920, Ernst Gagliardi from Zurich, a leading historian of his time, poetically praises the liberal triumph as Switzerland's 're-emergence among the truly independent states' and her regaining 'civilising equality' with other nations, even a fulfilment of Zwingli's programme, because Catholicism and especially ultramontanism are definitively rolled back.[36] Yet in 1937, when Gagliardi rewrites his text, he insists on the economic situation which imposes political modernisation against traditional particularism.[37] What has happened? The rapid economic development of the nineteenth century had often been described, but never in relation to 1848.[38] However, in

1912 the later famous economist and diplomat William Rappard, then a student at Harvard, first reflects on the 'economic factor in the generation of modern Swiss democracy'.[39] In 1928, the year of his death, Eduard Fueter publishes a history of Switzerland since 1848, with a first chapter describing the economic structures in the middle of the century. Before going on to discuss the political institutions of the highly praised Constitution, he deliberately first presents the 'new creations concerning commerce and economy'.[40] Gagliardi's changed view is obviously due to Fueter, and another admirer of Fueter's, Hans Nabholz, writes in 1944 a fundamental article about 'the rise of the federal state from the perspective of economic history', where he puts forward the view that the adaptation to economic change was the 'first and continually effective stimulus for constitutional reform' but admits that only the political struggle finally led to it.[41] Analysing discussions about customs duty, Walther Rupli in 1949 concludes that the economic and political motives leading to the new state carried equal weight.[42]

After Nabholz, the economic aspects of 1848 are stressed in many other books[43] and the rise of National Socialism and endemic anti-parliamentarianism in Switzerland also gives another impulse to national historiography. In 1938, Werner Näf states that Switzerland was the first European state to become a democratic republic as a result of the country's past and characteristics; here, 'the individualistic revolution was a revival, not a rupture'.[44]

The experience of the Second World War strengthens not only the democratic identity, but sharpens sensitivity for the victims and tensions of 1848. The direct line, be it political or economic, that earlier historiography drew from the Enlightenment to the liberal apotheosis of 1848 and that has, in 1948, one of its last heralds in Gottfried Guggenbühl,[45] is openly questioned by Edgar Bonjour after the war, although in an earlier synthesis he himself gave quite a traditional, rather undifferentiated picture.[46] In 1948, Bonjour stresses the divergence of interests and points out that in such a complex situation, many alternative solutions remained possible. Thus the new Constitution is no longer a child of the liberal *Weltgeist*, but a stroke of luck followed by national reconciliation.[47] Bonjour sees the *Bruderkrieg* as a catastrophe, but praises the moderation of the victors; still, his real sympathy lies with the conservative mediators of Basle, the 'voice of conscience' among the factiousness, to whom Bonjour dedicates a specific piece of research.[48] This distance from the liberal tradition is partly explained by the national union during the Second World War that left little place for century-old antagonisms and little respect for civil wars; on the other hand, the warnings of such brilliant conservatives as Jacob Burckhardt became horribly true: the sovereign people, so cherished by the radicals, democratically elected Hitler in Germany and turned into a mass and a populace under his rule.

These new aspects of 1848 were canonised in 1948 with the official book of the jubilee, a vade-mecum for every interested citizen entitled *Swiss Democracy 1848 to 1948*, with Ferdinand Hodler's Tell on the frontispiece and an introduction by Enrico Celio, the President of the Federal Council. Celio compares the Constitution of 1848 to those of 1798, 1803 and 1815 and insists from the beginning that it is the only one which is completely Swiss in origin and content. Celio, a member of the Catholic conservative party, does not mention the Sonderbund War, but speaks of 1848 as a reform which set the country free from humiliating foreign influence. 'Be and remain true to your character' is the exhortation of the highest representative of Switzerland; be faithful to republican freedom, Swiss democracy, independence and neutrality which all are older than the liberal revolutions of the past two centuries. If we can believe E. Abderhalden in the same book, the new Constitution even 'corresponds in all decisive regulations to the nature and the needs of the people and the cantons and is a true masterpiece of political insight'. With Celio's and Abderhalden's words, the Constitution becomes the natural link between the glorious past of all Swiss and modern democracy as the result of a virtuous and harmonious people – it is a typical milestone of the Swiss *Sonderfall* which has nothing comparable in the universe.[49] This is a view which is shared by other important members of Celio's conservative party; the losers of 1848 have accepted that the 'transition from the federal union to the federal state was necessary to preserve the country'.[50]

Among the semi-official celebrators of the jubilee in 1948, we find three authors we have already mentioned: Nabholz, Huber and Rappard. Unlike the harmonious politicians, Hans Nabholz chooses strong words: a fight between ideologies (*Weltanschauung*) led to a revolution, and the new Constitution forged national consciousness.[51] Nabholz shares the pride that the democratic constitutional state of 1848 resisted the dictatorships in neighbouring countries with Max Huber who, at the official celebration in Zurich, praises 1848 as an expression of the century-old Swiss thirst for freedom. Yet, according to Huber, this freedom must constantly be asserted and defended, in 1848 as in his own dangerous times. In the age of totalitarianism, Huber sees the liberal Constitution as a means of defending individual freedom against the overwhelming state: through participation, guaranteed personal rights, checks and balances, the federative structure of the state.[52] William Rappard also thinks gratefully that the 'natural solution' of 1848 not only corresponds to the necessities of that critical time but also to the needs of later generations and even to the eternal requirements of the Swiss people which somehow has itself given birth to the Constitution in its 'truly Swiss spirit'.[53]

Among the leading Swiss intellectuals who raised their voices in 1948, Karl Schmid, Professor of German literature at the Federal Institute of Technology (ETH), was pensive rather than emotional. He argued that it was nothing short of a miracle that the state established in 1848 had lasted 100 years. He warns those who like to talk about 'our' achievements as if those of their ancestors were their own deeds. Have the Swiss been faithful to the Constitution of 1848? According to Schmid, the central state has grown in an unliberal, 'socialist' direction, reducing individual freedom, yet it attempts to protect the petty people of the lower classes and the whole nation itself in its fight against totalitarian states abroad. Would the liberals of 1848 agree with the foreign policy of their successors which is entrenched resistance rather than devoted sacrifice? What they understood by neutrality was prudence and readiness, willingness to fight with arms if necessary, and they would agree with that part of modern Swiss politics, but they would be suspicious about its material gains and not forget its moral aspects.[54]

Corresponding to the national union during and after the war which included the Socialists in fighting off the Nazi and Communist threats, the moderate left also participated in all these celebrations. Yet there were symptomatic intellectual and journalistic polemics about the meaning of 1848: while Socialists often claim to be the true heirs of the (radical) movement of the 1840s, the Freisinn angrily counters that there has been liberal continuity within its own party for at least the last 120 years. This position can imply criticism against Fueter's and others' materialist interpretation of 1848, which is still considered to be the idealistic child of liberal convictions. The ideological background at the beginning of the Cold War is even more obvious in another respect: for the liberals, 1848 means the definite end of a revolutionary era, because a fair constitution was established; on the other hand, the Socialists interpret 1848 as a revolution which does not necessarily have to be the last one.[55] This view goes back to Robert Grimm, one of the eminent leaders of the party, who, imprisoned as a leader during the general strike of 1918, wrote his *History of Switzerland in its Class Conflicts*, following the tradition of historical materialism. He explains the formation of the federal state as the 'bourgeois revolution' against aristocracy, a conflict that could only be resolved through 'raw violence', which in Grimm's own days became so frightening for the bourgeois. The defeated guerrillas of 1845 changed their methods and started a 'legalised revolution' with the strength of a national army, by which means they brought to an end their struggle of 50 years for a modern state and a unified economic area. Grimm praises the courage and the initiative of the former radicals, so different – according to him – from his contemporaries. Yet their Constitution was coined by the conservatism of the petty bourgeoisie that dominated the social structure of the country. Now that this structure has changed so much, the future will belong to the working class and international revolution.[56]

In his later political life Grimm was to moderate his prophecies, but the Socialists' claim for the heritage of 1848 endured, as is demonstrated by writers like Max Frisch and Peter Bichsel. Bichsel thanks the liberals to whom he believes he owes his personal freedom much more than to William Tell: 'they wanted to impose the idea of a state, not only economic interests'. The Constitution of 1848 was the work of the opposition, of the left, which, according to Bichsel, is one reason why their liberal 'successors' prefer the memory of 1291 to that of 1848.[57] In Frisch's *Stiller* (1954), the protagonist White/ Stiller regrets that the conservative and indolent Swiss do not want their future, but their past. The last time they had a real project, a real aim must have been around 1848: a great, truly lively and creative epoch. In *achtung: Die Schweiz*, published around the same time (1955), Frisch, together with Lucius Burckhardt and Markus Kutter, again demands that Switzerland should have a goal and proposes a 'new town': such a design for the future is worthy of the memory of 1848, where political parties made a Utopia become reality.[58]

Such judgements went on haunting the political foes who are described as mere executors of the liberal revolution and marked their interpretation of the nineteenth century, too. The antagonists of 1848, conservatives and liberals, have already come together since at least 1891 in their anti-Socialism which – in spite of some sympathies, even in bourgeois circles, for the USSR which defeated Hitler's troops – dominated Switzerland again after 1948. It is quite symbolic that in a very popular, illustrated history of Switzerland, published several times from 1961 onwards, the modern period is covered by a Catholic from St Gallen who taught in the quite orthodox college of Schwyz. Emil Spiess wrote impressive studies on the two fascinating authors I. P. V. Troxler and G. J. Baumgartner, both torn between Catholic faith and liberal convictions. Spiess not only shows much sympathy for the legal position of the losers of 1847; in the middle of the Cold War, he sees a decisive role for German emigrants and Communists for the radical cause in the Sonderbund crisis and cites extensively Friedrich Engels's article 'The Swiss Civil War' published on 14 November 1847. What Spiess declares to be an impartial position has become even more than in Bonjour's case very close to the liberal–conservative *juste milieu* which Spiess still criticises for its inefficiency in avoiding the civil war. Still, he praises the importance of the conservatives for the new Constitution that meets with Spiess's approval: without their resistance to revolution and to the radicals, the particularist tradition would not have made much impression on modern Switzerland.[59]

Thus, in the second half of our century, Swiss historiography chooses a rather conservative middle way in judging the events of 1847 and 1848[60] and appraising the new Constitution, but far from the liberal enthusiasm of the earlier decades and in a way in the tradition of Jeremias Gotthelf who, once a young liberal, had become a sceptical conservative.[61] By now, the confessional strife no longer influences an individual's judgement: Hanno Helbling, a Protestant from the Engadin, whose scholarly research had concentrated on medieval (and thus Catholic) Italian thinking before he became the liberal *Neue Zürcher Zeitung* specialist for the Vatican and later director of its *Feuilleton*, states in 1963 that 'guilt was uniformly distributed' between the two camps. For Helbling, 1848 is the end of a 'period of searching' followed by the 'responsibility of finding'; what was found should last and yet was open to change, to reform.[62] Thus the regeneration and Sonderbund issue has definitely become a historical matter, the judgements no longer depend on one's confession or political affiliation but rather on one's idea about legitimate ways of change or progress in history. As the Swiss political system has definitely become a search for compromises since the *Zauberformel* of 1959, a distant and barely involved historian like Georges Andrey in the 1983 *History of Switzerland and the Swiss* can see the difficult transition from 1798 to 1848 moderated by many compromises which helped to support the revolutionary changes.[63] Thus, the 1840s become an important step, but not the only one, within a successful and fairly smooth path to modernisation in politics, society and economics. According to the general shift in postwar historiography, the structural force of the industrial revolution is generally considered more important than the bayonets of Dufour's troops.

In a way surprisingly, it is a historian of economic history who has just recently given another turn to the interpretation of the 1840s. Hansjörg Siegenthaler has not ignored the fact that the new state made an industrial upturn possible in the second half of the nineteenth century but that uncontested consequence of 1848 may not necessarily be a reason for the people acting in the first half of the century. Based on a 'kulturalistisch aufgerüstete ökonomische Handlungstheorie', an adaptation of the economist's 'rational choice' theory to historical science, Siegenthaler wonders what makes individuals act together with other individuals to promote change, even if it means costs and sacrifices for them. They only do that if they need each other and they need each other if they are in an 'epistemological crisis', if they have lost former certitude. Such a fight for the 'sources of truth' was fought until the decision of 1847 and 1848 brought new 'belief in the rules'.[64] This interpretation means that the existing economic reasons for a stronger union in Switzerland did not motivate individuals to fight for it. Siegenthaler's position has been further developed by several of his pupils but has also encountered opposition from 'materialistic' historians.[65] As a result of these recent debates, however, one can say that Siegenthaler's position has convinced most of his fellow historians.

We can briefly sum up this overview of 150 years of historiography as follows:

- the losers of 1847 deploring the broken traditional law;
- the 'idealistic' winners rejoicing about a successful liberal *Weltgeist*, but moderating their triumphant outbreaks at least from 1891 onwards;

- Grimm's Socialist version of a determined, but materialistically presented progress through a first, bourgeois revolution;
- the 'materialist turn' within liberal historiography since Fueter highlighted the economic aspects of 1848;
- the organic interpretation during the confrontation with the Nazis and Communism, pointing out that the harmonious solution of 1848 accorded with the true nature of the Swiss and was free from foreign influence;
- the neo-conservative shift during the Cold War, sceptical about an age of revolutions;
- finally, an interpretation based on economic theories of rational acting, typical of our times of globalisation and a preponderance of economy in theory and in practice.

Let me finish with some short observations about other recent approaches to 1848. As the speech of a leading Catholic politician at a commemoration of 1848 shows, the bad feeling on the part of the conservative losers is not as far away as one might think.[66] This points to the discontinuity, the rupture of the 50 years from 1798 to 1848 which put an end to the Swiss Confederation their ancestors had wanted. Most historians nowadays emphasise that rupture too; if they belong to the left, they often combine their appraisal for the new federal state with the claim already mentioned that the Socialists are its true heirs.[67] From a feminist point of view, the exclusion of women during the period of nation-building has been interpreted as a result of the influential men's clubs as a basis of the liberal revolution; such political associations provided the shelter of a family without depending on women because new members did not have to be born but were co-opted according to social rules.[68] Finally, there is a public debate about similarities between the Swiss nation-building in the nineteenth century and the further development of institutions within the EU. Surprisingly, there are even prominent authors of the nineteenth century who prophesied a European federal state according to the Swiss model. Thus, the jurist Johann Caspar Bluntschli, a leader of the conservative coup of 1839 in Zurich, stated: 'When one day the ideal of the future (to which Switzerland has shown the way) is realised, then the international Swiss nationality may dissolve into the big European community. It will not have lived in vain nor without glory.'[69]

Notes

1. Joachim Remak, *A Very Civil War. The Swiss Sonderbund War of 1847* (Boulder/San Francisco/Oxford, 1993).
2. In this survey, which constitutes the first part of this essay, I will only mention the literature when I quote directly. For further information see classic works such as Edgar Bonjour, *Die Gründung des schweizerischen Bundesstaates* (Basle, 1948) or Erwin Bucher, *Die Geschichte des Sonderbundskrieges* (Zurich, 1966). Many recent approaches are brought together in the books mentioned in note 3 and in Andreas Ernst *et al.* (eds), *Revolution und Innovation. Die konfliktreiche Entstehung des schweizerischen Bundesstaates von 1848*, Die Schweiz 1798–1998: Staat – Gesellschaft – Politik, vol. 1 (Zurich, 1998); Urs Altermatt *et al.* (eds), *Die Konstruktion einer Nation. Nation und Nationalisierung in der Schweiz, 18–20. Jahrhundert*, Die Schweiz 1798–1998: Staat – Gesellschaft – Politik, vol. 4 (Zurich, 1998); see also Thomas Christian Müller, 'Die Schweiz 1847–49. Das vorläufige, erfolgreiche Ende der "demokratischen Revolution"?', in: Dieter Dowe *et al.* (eds), *Europa 1848. Revolution und Reform*, Forschungsinstitut der Friedrich-Ebert-Stiftung. Reihe Politik- und Gesellschaftsgeschichte, vol. 48 (Bonn, 1998), pp. 283–326. I have described the revolutionary period as it was reflected in the commentaries of the leading liberal newspaper in *Vom Sonderbund zum Bundesstaat. Krise und Erneuerung 1798–1848 im Spiegel der NZZ* (Zurich, 1998).
3. See Alfred Kölz, *Neue schweizerische Verfassungsgeschichte. Ihre Grundlinien vom Ende der Alten Eidgenossenschaft bis 1848* (Berne, 1992), pp. 227–300; Albert Tanner and Thomas Hildbrand (eds), *Im Zeichen der Revolution. Der Weg zum schweizerischen Bundesstaat 1798–1848* (Zurich, 1997), especially the contributions of Albert Tanner, '"Alles für das Volk". Die liberalen Bewegungen von 1830/31', pp. 51–74 and 'Das Recht auf Revolution. Radikalismus – Antijesuitismus – Nationalismus', pp. 113–37 and Marco Jorio, '"Wider den Park mit dem Teufel". Reaktion und Gegenwehr der Konservativen', pp. 139–60.
4. See *Neue Zürcher Zeitung*, 22 January 1846, entitled 'Über Volkssouveränität' referring to the earlier debate 'ob das Volk der Souverän sei oder ob dieser in dem Rathe der Stellvertreter des Landes gesucht werden müsse' which has now become the question, 'ob das Volk ein unumschränkter, absoluter oder aber ein konstitutioneller Oberherr sein solle'. The editor, Luigi Ercole Daverio, sees it as 'eine Frage über die Schranken der oberherrlichen Gewalt, ob nämlich die Verfassung auch als eine Schranke für den Souverän anzusehen sei oder nicht'. His conclusion is the opposite of Druey's (see note 5), for he says that 'da wo die Stellvertreter eines Volkes unter Ratifikationsverbehalt deselben eine Verfassung erlassen, hat dieselbe eine so bindende Kraft, als irgend ein vertrag, den Einzelne unter sich abgeschlossen und mit Namensunterschriften versehen haben. [. . .] Die Ansicht dagegen, es sei das Volk ein durchaus selbständiges, unabhängiges Individuum, das nach Belieben Vorsätze fassen, abändern oder unerfüllt lassen kann, müssen wir entschieden verwerfen, als unbegründet in der Theorie und verderblich in der Praxis.'

5. Henri Druey in his *Nouvelliste Vaudois*, 5 November 1844, cited by Edgar Bonjour, 'Die Gründung des schweizerischen Bundesstaates' (Basle, 1948), p. 198, says that 'le radicalisme reconnaît au peuple le droit d'exercer sa souveraineté à chaque instant, comme il le veut, sa volonté suprême ne pouvant pas être liée par la constitution qui est un acte de cette volonté et non un contrat.'

6. Tanner, *Das Recht auf Revolution* (see note 3), p. 122.

7. As quoted in the *NZZ*, see Maissen, *Vom Sonderbund* (see note 2), p. 151.

8. Philipp Anton von Segesser to Andreas Heusler (9 February 1848), in Von Segesser/Heusler, *Briefwechsel*, edited by Victor Conzemius, prepared by Heidi Bossard-Borner, vol. 1 (Zurich/Einsiedeln/Cologne, 1983), p. 494.

9. See Edgar Bonjour, *Das Schicksal des Sonderbunds in zeitgenössischer Darstellung* (Aarau, 1947); for the contemporary and later authors see also Edgar Bonjour and Richard Feller, *Geschichtsschreibung der Schweiz vom spätmittelalter zur Neuzeit*, vol. 2 (Basle/Stuttgart, 1979).

10. Constantin Siegwart-Müller, *Der Sieg der Gewalt über das Recht in der Schweizerischen Eidgenossenschaft* (Altdorf, 1866), pp. v–xi (Vorwort).

11. Joseph Balthasar Ulrich, *Der Bürgerkrieg in der Schweiz* (Einsiedeln, 1850), pp. iii–vi (Vorrede), 762–8.

12. Bernhard Meyer, *Über Annahme oder Verwerfung der neuen Bundesverfassung* (Zurich, 1848). See also Bonjour, *Gründung* (see note 2), p. 182.

13. Jakob Baumgartner, *Die Schweiz in ihren Kämpfen und Umgestaltungen von 1830 bis 1850*, vol. 1 (Zurich, 1853), p. vii; vol. 4, pp. 606–7.

14. Jakob Baumgartner, *Schweizerspiegel. Drei Jahre unter der Bundesverfassung von 1848* (Zurich, 1851), pp. vii, 235–44; see also Heidi Borner, *Zwischen Sonderbund und Kulturkampf. Zur Lage der Besiegten im Bundesstaat von 1848*, Luzernische Historische Veröffentlichungen, vol. 11 (Lucerne, 1981), pp. 31–2.

15. Dr C. Weber (i.e. Niklaus Friedrich von Tschudi), *Der Sonderbund und seine Auflösung von dem Standpunkte einer nationalen Politik* (St Gallen, 1848), pp. 3–7, 36–7; see also Bonjour, *Schicksal* (see note 9), pp. 66–8.

16. Jakob Amiet, *Der siegreiche Kampf der Eidgenossen gegen Jesuitismus und Sonderbund* (Solothurn, 1848), cited in Bonjour, *Schicksal* (see note 9), p. 58.

17. J. Martin Rudolf, *Die Geschichte der Ereignisse in der Schweiz seit der Aargauische Klosteraufhebung 1841 bis zur Auflösung des Sonderbundes und zur Ausweisung der Jesuiten* (Zurich, 1848), pp. 489–95; see also Bonjour, *Schicksal* (see note 9), pp. 65–6.

18. See for example the woodcut *Alt und Jung* by Jakob Ziegler with Jakob Amiet's text, in *Illustrieter Schweizer Kalender* (Ziegler-Kalender, 1850), p. 17. Similarly the *Neue Zürcher Zeitung* celebrating the new Constitution on 14 September 1848 states that

über Berge und Thäler haben sich heute die Eidgenossen ihren Jubel zugedonnert; die wenigen, die in finsteres Schweigen sich hüllen, sollen unsere Freude nicht trüben. Keine Freudenfeuer dürfen heute von den Bergeshöhen herableuchten, von welchen die ersten Feuersignale der schweizerischen Freiheit erglänzten. Wohlan! die Reihe ist jetzt an den jüngern Söhnen der Freiheit. An diesen ist es nun, ihren ältern Brüdern die im Laufe der Jahrhunderte durch herrschsüchtige Magnaten und freiheitsfeindliche Priester ihnen verkümmerte Freiheit zu verkünden – und zu bringen. Von dem geistigen Drucke der neuen Gessler die Urstätte schweizerischer Freiheit zu befreien, wird nicht das letzte Bestreben der den neuen Bund freudig begrüssenden Eidgenossen sein.

19. For the denigration of the 'oligarchic' *ancien régime* see Andreas Würgler, *Die Legitimierung der Revolution aus den Unruhen des Ancien Régime durch die schweizerische Nationalhistoriographie des 19. Jahrhunderts*, in Ernst *et al.* (eds), *Revolution und Innovation* (see note 2), pp. 79–90.

20. For Tillier see Bonjour, *Schicksal* (see note 9), p. 72.

21. Guillaume-Henri Dufour, *Campagne du Sonderbund et événements de 1856*. *Précédé d'une notice biographique d'Edouard Sayous* (Neuchâtel/Geneva/Paris, 1876); see also Olivier Reverdin, *La guerre du Sonderbund vue par le Général Dufour, Juin 1847–Avril 1848*. *D'après des lettres et des documents inédits* (Geneva, 1948; reprinted 1997). Early historiographic praise of Dufour is found in Eusèbe-Henri Gaullieurs, *La Suisse en 1847* (Geneva, 1948); see Bonjour, *Schicksal* (see note 9), p. 69.

22. Peter Feddersen, *Geschichte der Schweizerischen Regeneration von 1840 bis 1848* (Zurich, 1867), pp. iii–v, 567, 582.

23. Karl Dändliker, *Geschichte der Schweiz* (Zurich, 1887), pp. 615, 654.

24. Johanes Dierauer, *Geschichte der Schweizerischen Eidgenossenschaft*, vol. 5 (Gotha, 1917), pp. 679, 686, 785–6.

25. Numa Droz, 'Die Wiedergeburt', in Paul Seippel (ed.), *Die Schweiz im neunzehnten Jahrhundert*, vol. 1 (Berne/Lausanne, 1899), pp. 275–6 where he says that 'die gemässigten Elemente, welche allein aufzubauen vermögen, hatten die Oberhand gewonnen. [. . .] Jetzt war das Werk der Wiedergeburt vollbracht. Die fremde Vormundschaft war gebrochen. Die Schweiz trat in eine neue Ära ihrer Geschichte ein'.

26. Theodor Curti, *Geschichte der Schweiz im 19. Jahrhundert* (Neuchâtel, 1901), p. 539.

27. Max Huber, *Der schweizerische Staatsgedanke* (Zurich, 1916), p. 13.

28. Nabholz, *Hundertjahrfeier* (see note 51), (referring to Huber); Ulrich Im Hof, *Vom Bundesbrief zur Bundesverfassung* (Rorschach, 1948), p. 164; Wolfgang von Wartburg, *Geschichte der Schweiz* (Munich, 1951), p. 205.

29. Joseph Hürbin, *Handbuch der Schweizer Geschichte*, vol. 2 (Stans, 1903), pp. 605–11.

30. Georg Kreis, *Der Mythos von 1291. Zur Entstehung des schweizerischen Nationalfeiertags* (Basle, 1991).

31. See also François de Capitani, 'Die Suche nach dem gemeinsamen Nenner – der Beitrag der Geschichtsschreiber', in François de Capitani and Georg Germann, *Auf dem Weg zu einer schweizerischen Identität 1848–1914. Probleme – Errungenschaften – Misserfolge* (Fribourg, 1987), pp. 25–35.

32. Georg Kreis, 'Das Verfassungsjubiläum von 1948', in *Jubiläen der Schweizer Geschichte 1798–1848–1998*, Studien und Quellen, vol. 24 (Berne, 1998), pp. 133–5.

33. Carl Hilty, *Die Bundesverfassungen der Schweizerischen Eidgenossenschaft* (Berne, 1891), pp. 402–7.
34. Eduard His, *Geschichte des neuern Schweizerischen Staatsrechts*, vol. 2 (Basle, 1929), pp. 773–4; vol. 3 (Basle, 1938).
35. Andreas Heusler, *Schweizerische Verfassungsgeschichte* (Basle, 1920), pp. 375–81.
36. Ernst Gagliardi, *Geschichte der Schweiz von den Anfängen bis zur Gegenwart*, first edition, vol. 2 (Zurich, 1920), pp. 426, 434. On p. 435 Gagliardi names the three historical sources of the new Constitution as 'alemannisches Streben nach Bewahrung der Volksfreiheit', 'Rousseausche Lehre von der Volkssouveränität' and 'das Beispiel Nordamerikanischer Union'.
37. Ernst Gagliardi, *Geschichte der Schweiz von den Anfängen bis zur Gegenwart*, 4th edition, vol. 3 (Zurich, 1939), pp. 1378–81 where he writes that 'Ökonomische Zwangsläufigkeit spielte beim Kampf um das neue Grundgesetz sonach eine entscheidende Rolle.' See also p. 1415.
38. See for example the third volume of Seippel's Swiss history (see note 25) which contains chapters on agriculture, industry, transport and the working-class movement.
39. William E. Rappard, *Le facteur économique dans l'avènement de la démocratie moderne en Suisse*, vol. 1, *L'agriculture à la fin de l'Ancien Régime* (Geneva, 1912). No further volumes published.
40. Eduard Fueter, *Die Schweiz seit 1848. Geschichte, Politik, Wirtschaft* (Zurich/ Leipzig, 1928), pp. 12–19, 39–43. Emil Dürr, *Neuzeitliche Wandlungen in der schweizerischen Politik. Historisch–politische Betrachtung über die Verwirtschaftlichung der politischen Motive und Parteien* (Basle, 1928), is another testimony to this new interest among historians for economic change, but as far as 1848 is concerned he accords more importance to politics than to economy (p. 22).
41. Hans Nabholz, 'Die Entstehung des Bundesstaates wirtschaftsgeschichtlich betrachtet', in *Mélanges offerts à Charles Gilliard* (Lausanne, 1944), pp. 574–90. See also Nabholz's obituary notice on Fueter in *Neue Zürcher Zeitung*, 2 December 1928, and Hans Conrad Peyer, 'Der Historiker Eduard Fueter. Leben und Werk', in *145. Neujahrsblatt zum Besten des Waisenhauses Zürich für 1982*, pp. 5–72, especially pp. 53 and 57.
42. Walther Rupli, *Zollreform und Bundesreform in der Schweiz 1815–1848. Die Bemühungen um die wirtschaftliche Einigung der Schweiz und ihr Einfluss auf die Gründung des Bundesstaates von 1848* (Zurich, 1959), pp. 206–7. See also Jean-François Bergier, *Die Wirtschaftsgeschichte der Schweiz* (Zurich, 1959), pp. 206–7. See also Jean-François Bergier, *Die Wirtschaftsgeschichte der Schweiz* (Zurich, 1983), p. 210 where he comments that 'die Industrialisierung hat, wenn auch spät, vermutlich mehr als jeder andere Faktor zur Einführung eines solchen [politischen, sozialen und institutionellen] Apparates beigetragen'.
43. See for example Karl Schib, *Illustrierte Schweizergeschichte für jedermann* (Zurich, 1944), pp. 179–81 and 'Vom Staatenbund zum Bundesstaat', in *Schweizerische Demokratie* (see note 49), pp. 26–7. See also Walter

Stampfli, 'Die Bundesverfassung von 1848 und die schweizerische Wirtschaft', in *Schweizerische Demokratie*, pp. 331–5.

44. Werner Näf, *Die Schweiz in Europa. Die Entwicklung des schweizerischen Staates im Rahmen der europäischen Geschichte* (Berne, 1938), pp. 57–8.

45. Gottfried Guggenbühl, *Geschichte der Schweizerischen Eidgenossenschaft*, vol. 2 (Erlenbach, 1948); see pp. 416–20, which cover the 'home-grown will' *(einheimischer Wille)* that in one of the 'luckiest' years of Swiss history, made possible the new Constitution, which included a 'considerable swissification' *(Verschweizerung)* of the American model.

46. Edgar Bonjour, *Geschichte der Schweiz im 19. und 20. Jahrhundert*, Geschichte der Schweiz, edited by Hans Nabholz *et al.*, vol. 2 (Zurich, 1938), pp. 433–62.

47. Bonjour, *Gründung* (see note 2), pp. 5–6.

48. Bonjour, *Schicksal* (see note 9), p. 73 and *Gründung* (see note 2), p. 152. For Basle see Bonjour, *Basels Vermittlung in den Sonderbundswirren* (Basle, 1948) which originally appeared in *Archiv des Historischen Vereins des Kantons Bern*, vol. 39 (Berne, 1948).

49. *Schweizerische Demokratie 1848–1948. Ein Jubiläumswerk*, edited by Arnold H. Schwengeler (Murten, 1948), pp. 13–16, 35. On p. 34 Abderhalden's explanation of the importance of the new Constitution is very like Celio's. He declares: 'sie überwand die im Sonderbundskrieg zum Ausdruck gekommenen Gegensätze und schuf als Abschluss und Krönung einer jahrhundertlangen Entwicklung aus einem schwerfälligen Bund selbständiger Staaten einen allen Anforderungen der Neuzeit gewachsenen Bundesstaat'.

50. Alphons Iten, President of the Swiss Ständerat, as cited in Kreis, *Verfassungsjubiläum* (see note 32), p. 160. Kreis discusses the official jubilees and the differences between the commemorative discourses of the different political parties.

51. Hans Nabholz, 'Zur Hundertjahrfeier der Bundesverfassung des Jahres 1848', in *Die Schweiz. Ein nationales Jahrbuch 19* (1948), pp. 3–16, especially pp. 3, 8, 11, 13.

52. Max, Huber, *Die Bundesverfassung von 1848 als Ausdruck schweizerischen Freiheitswillens*, Kantonal-Zürcherische Hundertjahrfeier der Bundesverfassung, 4 Juli 1948 (Zurich, 1948), pp. 14–25.

53. William E. Rappard, *Die Bundesverfassung der Schweizerischen Eidgenossenschaft 1848–1948* (Zurich, 1948), pp. 429–33.

54. Karl Schmid, 'Ein Jahrhundert Bundesstaat', in Schmid, *Zeitspuren. Aufsätze und Reden*, vol. 2 (Zurich/Stuttgart, 1967), pp. 32–41.

55. See details about the quarrel concerning an exhibition commemorating 1848 in Kreis, *Verfassungsjubiläum* (see note 32), pp. 164–7, and also pp. 148–50 for comment on the attempt by the Socialists to lay claim to the heritage of 1848.

56. Robert Grimm, *Geschichte der Schweiz in ihren Klassenkämpfen* (Berne, 1920), pp. 368–82, 405–7.

57. Peter Bichsel, *Des Schweizers Schweiz* (Frankfurt am Main, 1997), pp. 16–17 (first printed in 1969).

58. Max Frisch, *Stiller*, in *Gesammelte Werke in zeitlicher Folge*, vol. 3 (Frankfurt am Main, 1976), p. 596 and *achtung: Die Schweiz*, in *Gesammelte Werke*, p. 336. See also the recent thesis by Sonja Rüegg, *'Ich hasse nicht die Schweiz, sondern die Verlogenheit'. Das Schweiz-Bild in Max Frischs Werken 'Graf Öderland', 'Stiller' und 'achtung: die Schweiz' und ihre zeitgenössische Kritik* (Zurich, 1998), especially pp. 241, 312–14 and 389 (referring to a letter written in 1991) where the author remarks:

> Der Rekurs auf die Staatsgründer von 1848 zieht sich von *Stiller* über *achtung: Die Schweiz* durch bis zu dieser letzten öffentlichen Äusserung Frischs. [...] Mit der Berufung auf die Gründer von 1848 erinnert Frisch das heutige *Bürgertum*, das sich als Nachkomme der liberalen Gründerväter versteht, immer wieder [...] an ihr eigenes, ursprüngliches Versprechen und ihr Versagen davor.

59. Emil Spiess, *Das Werden des Bundesstaates und seine Entwicklung um modernen Europa*, Illustrierte Geschichte der Schweiz, vol. 3 (Einsiedeln/ Zurich/Cologne, 1961), pp. 155–7, 167–8, 184.
60. See also Peter Dürrenmatt, *Schweizer Geschichte*, vol. 2 (Zurich, 1976), pp. 641–78.
61. For Gotthelf see Albert Tanner, 'Vom "ächten Liberalen" zum "militanten" Konservativen. Jeremias Gotthelf im politischen Umfeld seiner Zeit', in Hanns Peter Holl and J. Harald Wäber, *'Zu schreien in die Zeit hinein.' Beiträge zu Jeremias Gotthelf/Albert Bitzius (1797–1854)* (Berne, 1997), pp. 11–59.
62. Hanno Helbling, *Schweizer Geschichte* (Zurich, 1963), pp. 130, 134.
63. George Andrey, 'Auf der Suche nach dem neuen Staat (1798–1848), in *Geschichte der Schweiz und der Schweizer* (Basle/Frankfurt am Main, 1986), p. 630. Ernst Bohnenblust, *Geschichte der Schweiz* (Erlenbach, 1974), p. 439 also calls the new Constitution a 'work of agreement, a compromise between the parties'. A similar scientific distance marks the contributions of Jean-Charles Biaudet and Erwin Bucher in *Handbuch der Schweizer Geschichte*, vol. 2 (Zurich, 1977), and Ulrich Im Hof, *Geschichte der Schweiz* (Stuttgart, 1974), pp. 106–9.
64. Hansjörg Siegenthaler, 'Supranationalität, Nationalismus und regionale Autonomie. Erfahrungen des schweizerischen Bundesstaates, Perspektiven der europäischen Gemeinschaft,' in *Traverse*, 3 (1994), pp. 117–40; see also Siegenthaler, 'Weg der Vernunft in die Modernität. Vom Kampf um die Quellen der Wahrheit zur Gründung des Bundesstaates', *Neue Zürcher Zeitung*, 27/28 June 1998, p. 71.
65. See in Ernst *et al.* (eds), *Revolution und Innovation* (see note 2), the contributions of Patrick Halbeisen and Margrit Müller, Christoph Guggenbühl and Thomas Christian Müller who defend one side of the question and of Hans Ulrich Jost and Cédric Humair who disagree.
66. Carlo Schmid (Landammann of Appenzell-Innerrhoden), 'Geschichte der Integration', in *Republikanisches Bankett der Neuen Zürcher Zeitung zum 150-Jahr-Jubiläum des Schweizerischen Bundesstaates. 26 Juni 1998. Die Reden im Wortlaut* (Zurich, 1998), pp. 9–10.

67. For example Josef Lang, who also contributed an article about the Catholic radicals to Ernst, *Revolution* (see note 2), pp. 259–70; see his statements in *MOMA, Monatsmagazin für neue Politik*, 12.97/1.98. See also Tobias Kästli, *Die Schweiz – eine Republik in Europa. Geschichte des Nationalstaats seit 1798* (Zurich, 1998).
68. Lynn Blattmann and Irène Meier (eds), *Männerbund und Bundesstaat. Über die politische Kultur der Schweiz* (Zurich, 1998).
69. Cited in Daniel Thürer, 'Die drei Paradoxe in der Verfassung von 1848. Über ihre Relevanz im Zeitalter der Globalisierung, *NZZ*, 27/28 June 1998, p. 69.

2
Contemporary Reactions to '1848' by Writers and Intellectuals

Rémy Charbon

The title of my essay is problematic in two ways, both in relation to the intellectuals and to the year. It is true that 1848 was a key year in Swiss history, but it also marks the end of a long period of intellectual, political and armed confrontation. In this respect, statements about this threshold year also relate to the whole historical process which preceded it. There is some justification in saying that the first half of the century was devoted to preparing what shaped the second half. Nonetheless, what Max Frisch's character Stiller noted a century later in prison is still appropriate. Stiller, who had left Switzerland because of the pettiness of the country, returned after a few years inspired by a feeling which can only be rendered by the old-fashioned word 'homesickness', with a false passport and a false name as Mr White, in disguise, as it were. For him, 'the last great and genuinely real period' for Switzerland were 'die sogenannten acht-undvierziger Jahre. Damals hatten sie einen Entwurf. Damals wollten sie, was es zuvor noch nie gegeben hatte, und freuten sich auf das Morgen, das Übermorgen. Damals hatte die Schweiz eine geschichtliche Gegenwart.'[1]

That brings me to the second problem. Stiller rightly uses the plural form. Neither the 'draft plan' nor its realisation was the work of a single individual of genius. Just as the Swiss federal state was founded suddenly and just as it had a lengthy period of preparation, so there were many people involved. Are they to be described as 'intellectuals'? And how could a Swiss intellectual of the mid-nineteenth century be characterised? Certainly not as a man of grandiose plans, as a 'prophet' or even as a kind of guru. There were only very few professional intellectuals at this time, and there was no 'caste' of intellectuals at all. A German traveller, who himself was later to settle for many years in Switzerland as a professor, observed with a certain consternation: 'Die Schweizer sind kein literaturmachendes Volk. Einerseits ist ihr Sinn zu praktisch, um sich viel mit Büchern abzugeben, andereseits verschlingt die politische Debatte die wenige Zeit, welche sie ihren Geschäften entziehen.'[2]

Typically, the chairs at the newly founded universities of Berne and Zurich were filled with Germans in the first instance. Anyone making public pronouncements in Switzerland, anyone putting forward political 'draft plans', anyone writing books usually was also by profession principally a politician or leader-writer for a political newspaper, or at least a minister of religion or a teacher. Swiss pragmatism mistrusted purely theoretical draft plans, and tested existing models for their viability so as to tailor them to specific requirements. Let me demonstrate this with an example. After the defeat of the Sonderbund, the way was clear for a new organisation for the state which would replace the Federation treaty of 1815. A commission, appointed by the Federal Diet, the only political forum in the loose federation of states, was given the task of drawing up a draft plan for a new constitution. Just a few weeks previously, the only Swiss philosopher of note in the first half of the nineteenth century, Ignaz Paul Vital Troxler of Lucerne, had once more sat down at his desk and had written a pamphlet with the programmatic title *Die Verfassung der Vereinigten Staaten Nordamerikas als Musterbild der Schweizerischen Bundesreform*. Twenty years before, Troxler had propagated the American bicameral system because only in this way could the interests of the individual and the collective be brought together, as well as the demands of the centralists seeking a federal state and those of the federalists seeking a confederation of states. At that time, he, and those who agreed with him, had had no success. In 1848 the situation was different. The victors of the Sonderbund war were among the former, the centralists, and the losers among the latter, the federalists. A solution to the problem could no longer be postponed.

Once more, Troxler demonstrated that the bicameral system was the only possibility 'daß alle Bundesglieder, klein und groß, ihre Zustimmung zur Bundesreform [...] erteilen'.[3] This consent was necessary, not simply because the cantons of the Sonderbund were still, despite their military defeat, fully entitled to vote at the Federal

Diet; it is also in the Swiss tradition to aim for consensus, or at least for a compromise acceptable to all. For a long time, the commission set up by the Diet was unable to achieve this. As the deliberations threatened to end in failure, a pupil of Troxler, who was moreover a representative of a Sonderbund canton, presented Troxler's pamphlet to some members of the commission, and on the following day the knot was unravelled and the bicameral system accepted.

The example is informative for several reasons. Firstly, because it is clear that the gap between political theory and political practice was very much less pronounced than, for example, in Germany; secondly, because the politicians were prepared to forget party political divisions and to propose a constitution drawn up by everyone; and finally, not least because Troxler, one of the few Swiss exercising an intellectual profession at the time (he was professor of philosophy in Berne), addressed himself as a matter of course to the practical political questions of the day. His pamphlet was anything but a long-winded treatise. Its main part was made up of a translation of the American Constitution. An easily comprehensible introduction setting forth historical and legal arguments and a brief discussion of the powers of the public prosecutor introduced this translation; there then followed statements by political theorists and a short conclusion, in which Troxler expounded the view that Switzerland certainly had the right to constitute herself politically according to her requirements, that is, not to feel herself bound by the Confederation Treaty of 1815 which had the blessing of the Great Powers. All things considered, it was a discussion paper for politicians.

The German observer already cited was right about the purely theoretical debates among intellectuals. But he misunderstands the significance of *public* political discussions about fundamentals. It is true that leading people discussed matters of principle among themselves, but less in learned treatises than in private letters which were directly linked to events of the day and did not require a systematic approach. But they preferred to address themselves to a politically interested public – and very many people were interested in political matters at that time – occasionally by means of popular pamphlets, but much more frequently in newspaper articles and speeches to the visitors at the big Swiss festivals. Here, over lunch in the great dining-hall where 3000–5000 people could sit together, political matters were discussed. At the Marksmen's Festival of 1844, for example, a fully worked-out draft for a new federal constitution was distributed and discussed. The debate was not conducted on a high theoretical level, but against that it was public and a plethora of voices joined in.

If you set out to analyse the reaction of the intellectuals to '1848' and to the preliminaries to the reconstruction of the state, you have therefore to study the leading articles of the newspapers of the time and the most detailed reports on mass meetings or contemporary literature. The German source got this point wrong too. It is true that in Switzerland there were no literary *salons* or circles, apart from the emigrant community, but there was literature as a public forum. Even our best writers were not too proud to speak out on the events of the day – simply as citizens without laying claim to belong to an elite.

Even during the period of armed hostilities, radical politicians, writers, journalists and intellectuals – in the limited sense already defined – had enthusiastically praised the dream of the 'new federation'. When it had become reality, there was really nothing more to add. The direct testimonies are then no longer of any interest since they simply repeat what was said years before. But soon a new component arrived: the 'new federation' was interpreted not so much as the fulfilment of radical wishes as the federation of *all* Swiss, that is to say, of the losers as well. From this perspective, the time of the civil war seems to be a necessary precondition for the fresh start (something which, incidentally, permitted people's own mistakes to be excused).

An early testimonial to this tacit understanding comes from an author who is completely unimportant as a writer, but who played an important part in the civil war. On the evening of the day when Berne was chosen as the federal capital, he has his *alter ego* reflect in front of the frieze of coats of arms in the Kornhauskeller in Berne:

> Bei dem Namen *Luzern* zogen vor meinem Geiste vorüber alle die bangen Stunden, die ich seit dem Unglücksjahr 1841 [als Luzern ultramontan wurde] dieses so schmählich getäuschten und mißbrauchten Volkes wegen erlitt [...]. Ich dankte in stillem Gebete der Vorsehung, die die Pläne der Verräter vereitelte [...]. Sie haben doch zu großen, zu ungeheuern Resultaten geführt, die so gehöhnten und geschmähten Freischarenzüge, und was sie

gewollt [...] ist endlich doch [...] durch die große Mehrheit des Schweizervolkes sanktioniert worden.[4]

Although they were permitted to feel that they were the victors, the radicals did not wallow in their triumph and carefully avoided any humiliation of their former opponents. In its first number after the foundation of the new state, the *Republikaner-Kalendar*, which had been extremely aggressive during the hostilities, mentioned in a retrospective review mainly examples of mutual help and personal friendship between members of the opposing armies. At that time, patriotism meant awareness of common ground and relativising one's own position to the point where it no longer required to be defended.

The most prominent example is Gottfried Keller, the most important German-speaking Swiss writer of the 1850s. Prior to 1848, he had written aggressive poems advocating struggle; afterwards, he became one of the spokesmen for reconciliation. In his first novel, *Der grüne Heinrich*, published between 1853 and 1855, the main character returns to Switzerland in 1844 after a long period of residence in Germany. He himself does not live to see 1848; but the narrator interprets events in a quite Hegelian fashion. Thesis and antithesis are presented as the precursors of a synthesis which reconciles opposites in a higher wholeness and so makes the question of guilt redundant:

Diese vermummten Zivilkrieger wollten für sich nichts, weder Beute noch Kriegsruhm, noch Beförderung holen, sondern zogen einzig für den reinen Gedanken aus; als sie daher allein an dem Fluche der Ungesetzlichkeit und offenen Vertragsbrüchigkeit untergingen, trat der noch seltsamere Fall ein, daß sie sich nicht ihrer Tat zu schämen brauchten und doch eingestehen durften, es sei gut, daß sie nicht gelungen, indem ohne den tragischen Verlauf der Freischarenzüge der Sonderbund nicht jene energische Form gewonnen hätte, die den schließlichen Sieg der legalen und ruhigen Freisinnigen herausgefordert und ermöglicht hat.[5]

A few years later, Keller returned to the theme in his story *Das Fähnlein der sieben Aufrechten*. The story is set at the Marksmen's Festival at Aarau in 1849. Here, in this former vassal state of Berne, which in

1798 had been for a short period the capital of the Helvetic Republic and since 1803 had been the capital of a new canton run by the liberals, Swiss marksmen met to celebrate the new state and to set a seal on reconciliation with their former opponents and to integrate them once and for all. Keller portrays the marksmen's festival of a very small group; it consists of seven old men who had all been active radicals during the period of hostilities. But now the quarrel is forgotten; the journey to Aarau is to be the 'Schlußvergnügen' of their 'politischen Lebensabend'.[6] The veterans are preoccupied with one worry only: not one of them feels able to hold the obligatory speech of welcome. The political slogans which they know from the time of struggle are no longer appropriate to the new era. Finally, the son of one of them assumes the task. The symbolic significance is clear: the old men have acted, now they may, indeed ought to, stay silent and rejoice at what has been achieved. The young people, who must provide substance for this political *form*, have the floor. Beneath the Swiss flag, the young orator finally becomes engaged to the daughter of another of the seven; founding a family and founding a state are two ways of expressing the same thing, the union of differing parts to one whole which is more than the sum of its parts.

It is appropriate to this desire for reconciliation that several authors, both conservative and radical, dispense with aggressive texts in the new editions of their works. Of course, there were also others. It was not only in the Sonderbund cantons that a certain reserve persisted for a long time. The most important author besides Keller, Jeremias Gotthelf from Berne (whose real name was Alber Bitzius), not only looked wrathfully on modern developments, but even stepped up his attacks on the liberal state. In his literary works, he made statements about the federal state only *en passant*, in a few malicious digs at individual federal councillors and at the institutions of the federal state in general. He was more forthright in his non-literary texts and in private letters: 'Die Despotie fängt an zu wachsen aus der Freiheit heraus auf abscheuliche Weise. Mit der Gerechtigkeit wird heillos Schindluder getrieben, und eidgenössische Repräsentanten legen eine Lügenfertigkeit und Schamlosigkeit an den Tag, daß es einem ordentlich die Haare zu Berge stellt.'[7]

Previously he had not much concerned himself with the Federation as a whole. His area of influence was the canton of Berne. In 1846, a radical government had been elected here. Gotthelf attacked it and the modern state ruled by law in general in a manner which was often simply intemperate. Already in his early works, the morally despicable characters had also been supporters of the radical party; now a direct link is postulated and the radical state portrayed as institutionalising what is repellent and as being a hotbed of criminals and cheats. Both his last two novels in fact deal with nothing other than the destruction of human lives by radicalism. The abstract order of the modern state which puts administrative decrees in place of care, which brings profit only to those who can exploit it unscrupulously for their own ends, the new, parasitical class of officials which is concerned solely with its own advantage and not with the well-being of the people, the reduction of social care to formulas and anonymity – these things were a thorn in the side of Gotthelf who had formerly been a liberal: 'Der Doktor [a voice of reason] tat auseinander, wie ein Land unglücklich werden müsse, wo Fleiss und Sparsamkeit nichts helfen, wo unter Schein Rechtens die tüchtigsten Leute um ihre Sache gebracht würden, förmlich ausgesogen werden könnten unter den Augen der ganzen Welt, ohne dass ihnen geholfen werde.'[8]

Gotthelf did not hesitate to pillory individual federal councillors as profiteers without conscience, bent only on their own advantage and leading the populace by the nose. Yet it would be quite wrong to characterise Gotthelf as a reactionary. He was still an opponent of the aristocracy and representative of a moderate liberalism which, however, no longer existed in political reality. Even more surprising is the fact that, in essential points, his analysis is identical to that of Karl Marx and Friedrich Engels. In the year in which the Swiss state was founded, the *Manifest der kommunistischen Partei*, written in exile in London, appeared. In the dissolution of the 'buntscheckigen Feudalbande, die den Menschen an seinen natürlichen Vorgesetzten knüpften',[9] the Communists and Gotthelf saw the origin of modern moral breakdown. Their conclusions are of course entirely different. Not the dictatorship of the proletariat, but awareness of the 'natural', and that meant that for the minister of religion, God-given relationships between humans, and the return to small, easily comprehensible structures can indicate a way out of the crisis. In a novel which appeared in 1850, *Die Käserei in der Vehfreude*, he portrayed a model of such a community with the example of a village which has decided to set up a co-operative cheese-making plant. The way in which the interests of the individual farms, which are to remain autonomous as far as possible, are balanced against those of the whole community, is obviously for him a counter-model to the organisation of the federal state.

Gotthelf was one of the first authors to see the connection between industrialisation and liberalism. In previous works, he had still judged the virtues of the industrial age to be positive – hard work, readiness to expand one's knowledge and to accept innovations. As the consequences became clear to him, he changed direction, without, however, abandoning his basically republican attitude.

It is surprising that the other authors who have been mentioned so far did not see this connection between liberalism and industrialisation. Switzerland was at the time far from being a mountain state off the beaten track. Certain regions of Switzerland were, immediately following the industrialised regions of England, among the earliest and most highly industrialised areas in the world. But almost all intellectuals saw only the political and patriotic component, and not the economic one. Among the exceptions along with Gotthelf is an author who is today forgotten but who at the time was known as the writer of a popular history of Switzerland and of some folksongs: Josef Anton Henne, a radical Catholic. It is not by chance that he came from a region which was marked early on by the textile industry. In 1851, on the occasion of the 500th anniversary of the accession of Zurich to the Confederation, he wrote a poem in seven cantos which, after an extensive historical review, moves into an appraisal of the cost exacted by the industrial age. At the first World Exhibition in London, Switzerland was also represented:

> Zu London vor Aller Augen liegt jetzt in bunter Pracht
> Zum Staunen ausgebreitet, was des Schweizers Sinn erdacht.[10]

There is no doubt that the internationalisation of trade and industry was made easier by the liberal state. For that reason, the industrialists almost without exception sided with the radicals. But since the radicals also represented the interests of the lower classes against the old liberals and conservatives, it was only later that class conflicts arose in Switzerland. The early Communist effusions of Wilhelm Weitling found a certain, if scarcely enthusiastic resonance, but the rational analysis of Karl Marx did not.

It seems, during the first years after 1848, as if people in Switzerland were so busy consolidating the new state and overcoming the shadows of the political past, that reflections on the future and on the phenomenon of relentless industrialisation simply evoked no interest. But events in Europe as a whole also had surprisingly little echo. Naturally, the revolutions in neighbouring countries were reported in the newspapers; but that was about all. It seems to me that an episode from the festival of reconciliation in Aarau in 1849 already mentioned is typical. At the same time as thousands of marksmen were gathering to bring the Swiss revolution to a happy close, on the other side of the border, in the Grand Duchy of Baden, an attempt at revolution was being crushed. An emissary from the revolutionaries appeared in Aarau, drew an emotional picture of the poverty and misery of the people and requested help. Augustin Keller, formerly a spokesman for the radicals, had no answer other than that the hands of the Swiss were tied: 'Wir können nicht [helfen], weil wir zu klein, – und wir dürfen nicht, weil wir zu große Verantwortung auf uns nehmen würden, gegenüber unserer eigenen Zukunft, gegenüber Weib und Kind, gegenüber unserer Freiheit, ja sogar gegenüber ganz Europa.'[11]

Only unity and persistence could help their 'German brothers'. Just as, in the period before 1848, radicals from half of Europe were enthusiastically welcomed, support was readily provided for them and they were even saved from their persecutors by being granted citizenship, so, after the foundation of the state, there was much reticence. That held good too in political practice. When the refugees from Baden came into Switzerland in their thousands, they were readily granted asylum, but were deported as quickly as possible to other countries. The reason was not simply indifference. It was wise to be prudent, because the attention of the European great powers was again turning in increasing measure to Switzerland. The founding of the federation had to some extent occurred in the shadow of the revolutionary year, but now the princes' courts were looking suspiciously at Switzerland, which – and this must not be forgotten – was the only republic in a Europe of monarchies, if one or two city republics are disregarded. Perhaps for this reason, there were efforts first of all to create an internal equilibrium and momentarily to exclude wider perspectives. Thus there was distinct reticence about declarations and political manifestations which could be interpreted as revolutionary.

Beyond journalists' reports, I know of no thorough-going discussion of the revolutions in the first years after 1848. In 1830, it had been different, perhaps because Switzerland was then bringing in her own reforms – the introduction of liberal principles in some cantons – in the wake of the upheavals in Paris, whereas in 1848 she was leading the field.

A certain stagnation is unmistakable, and that also perhaps explains the backward-looking attitude of the intellectuals and writers, their reluctance – despite the suppression of the 1848 revolutions – to address the changes in the times brought about by industrialisation and proletarianisation. Politically, the radicals were for the moment satisfied with themselves, although not all of their wishes had been fulfilled; there was still the matter of breathing life into the Constitution. The conservatives for their part were discovering that federalism, still clearly distinct, was offering them opportunities to realise in the cantons what was not possible at federal level. It was only a few years later that fresh impulses came. One of the first came from a young lawyer, Caspar Aloys Bruhin, who called the consensus of 1848 into question as declaring a false peace. In 1853 there appeared his 'Swiss novel', *Arnold*, which takes severely to task the self-satisfied habits of the radical politicians who became federal councillors and which even insinuates that they are secretly in league with reaction. Instead of the state of the *Wortfreisinnigen*, the task was to set up a 'wahren Volksstaat',[12] which could then really serve as a model for Europe. In other words, he was attacking the legitimacy of the liberal state at its roots. But for the time being his philippics resounded unheard; it was not until a decade later that the time was ripe for a movement for basic democracy (in which Bruhin then played a leading part). But even Bruhin rejects Marxist Socialism because in Switzerland a distinction between 'capitalists' and 'workers' was meaningless. The image of a single people created largely by writers and journalists was still too powerful.

A final question remains open: is there an echo of Swiss matters abroad? I can be brief. From the period itself, apart from newspaper reports and diplomatic documents, there is surprisingly little evidence. That may be due to the fact that, in all the countries neighbouring Switzerland, revolutionary movements were also taking place in 1848 and that the intellectuals interested in politics were occupied with their own affairs. An exception to this was formed by those politicians in opposition who had gone into exile before the

European year of revolution and who were now living in a country which was not directly affected by the upheavals. Ferdinand Freiligrath, a colleague of Karl Marx and Friedrich Engels, had stayed in Switzerland in 1845; as a consequence, he devoted his attention to the war of the Sonderbund. Its outcome was for him synonymous with the victory of progress over reaction and was a beacon for the whole of Europe.

When the revolution broke out in Paris in January 1848, he wrote a poem which in the very first line contains a historical prophecy (which did not in the event come to pass): 'Im Hochland fiel der erste Schuß / Im Hochland wider die Pfaffen'[13] – the first shot, that is, of a revolution throughout Europe which would sweep away the feudal regimes. And it was only this perspective which was important for him; the ensuing verses treat merely of the fighting at the Paris street-barricades, of the abdication of the French king and of potentates' fear of revolution.

Less enthusiastically, with a certain reserve even, but nonetheless in sympathy with the Swiss, Friedrich Engels who, just at the time when the parliament began its work was staying in Berne, reported for the *Neue Rheinische Zeitung* the consolidation of the new state. He reproached the National Council for being unable to agree immediately on the presidency, with 'echt schweizerischer Uneinigkeit und Kleinigkeitsträumerei',[14] and on the other hand, he advised the Germans to pay attention to events in Switzerland because 'was die Schweizer denken, sagen, tun und treiben, kann nur in sehr kurzer Frist als Vorbild vorgehalten werden'.[15]

The evidence thus shows that Swiss intellectuals and writers produced neither important theories before the foundation of the state nor comprehensive analyses afterwards. But they accompanied the development of the federal state and promoted it in many cases. With occasional poems and broadsheets – which I have been unable to discuss here – they contributed much to internal communication at critical moments of history and often even assumed political responsibility. On the other hand, politicians occasionally wrote verses and pamphlets, not from vanity, but because they saw in these forms of expression a different, perhaps greater potential for effect than in purely political argument. This kind of pragmatism seems to me to be characteristic of nineteenth-century Switzerland.

Translated by Malcolm Pender

Notes

1. Max Frisch, *Gesammelte Werke in zeitlicher Folge*, vol. 3 (Frankfurt am Main, 1976), p. 596.
2. Johannes Scherz, *Die Schweiz und die Schweizer* (Winterthur, 1845), p. 72.
3. Ignaz Paul Vital Troxler, *Die Verfassung der Vereinigten Staaten Nordamerikas als Musterbild der Schweizerischen Bundesreform* (Schaffhausen, 1848), p. 12.
4. Adrian von Arx, *Phantasieen [sic] im Berner Kornhauskeller* (Berne, 1849), pp. 11f.
5. Thomas Böning and Gerhard Kaiser (eds), *Gottfried Keller, Sämtliche Werke in sieben Bänden*, vol. 2, *Der grüne Heinrich*. *Erste Fassung* (Frankfurt am Main, 1985), p. 885.
6. Gottfried Keller, *Sämtliche Werke*, vol. 5, *Züricher Novellen*, p. 246.
7. Rudolf Hunziker, Hans Bloesch *et al.* (eds), *Jeremias Gotthelf, Sämtliche Werke in 24 Bänden und 18 Ergänzungsbänden*, suppl. vol. 7 (Erlenbach-Zurich, 1911–77), p. 110 (to Abraham Emmanuel Fröhlich, 31 January 1848).
8. Jeremias Gotthelf, *Sämtliche Werke*, vol. XIV, *Erlebnisse eines Schuldenbauers*, pp. 310f.
9. Karl Marx/Friedrich Engels, *Manifest der Kommunistischen Partei* (Stuttgart, 1969), p. 16.
10. Josef Anton Henne, 'Die Sieben Zürich. Auf das Maifest 1851', in: Robert Weber (ed.), *Album vaterländischer Dichter auf Zürichs Bundesfeier* (Zurich, 1851), p. 49.
11. Augustin Keller, 'Ansprache am Schützenfest in Aarau 1849', in *Beschreibung des eidgenössischen Freischiessens abgehalten in Aarau vom 1. bis 8. Juli 1849* (Aarau/Thun, 1849), p. 26.
12. C[aspar] A[loys] Bruhin, *Arnold. Ein Schweizer Roman* (Berne, 1857), p. 74.
13. Ferdinand Freiligrath, 'Im Hochland fiel der erste Schuß', in: Ferdinand Freiligrath, *Neuere politische und soziale Gedichte* (Cologne [published privately], 1849), p. 39.
14. Friedrich Engels, 'Die neuen Behörden – Fortschritte in der Schweiz', in: Karl Marx/Friedrich Engels, *Werke*, vol. 6 (Berlin, 1959), p. 16.
15. Friedrich Engels, 'Der Nationalrat', in: Karl Marx/Friedrich Engels, *Werke*, vol. 6, p. 85.

3

How to Create a National Myth: Switzerland Reflected in its Contemporary Writing

Urs Bugmann

Switzerland is in crisis – in a deep identity crisis, to be precise. And this has not just been the case since Senator Alfonse M. D'Amato and American lawyers like Edward D. Fagan demanded that Switzerland admit its guilt and make reparation for its dealings during the Second World War, nor since Jewish organisations claimed compensation from a country that considered itself innocent and believed it had escaped the tangled web of world history unsullied with historical guilt. Nor did the crisis begin when security man Christoph Meili took papers from the shredding room of the Zurich branch of UBS (Union Bank of Switzerland), papers that were destined for destruction even though their content dealt with highly sensitive events in the 1930s and 1940s.

The roots of Switzerland's identity crisis lie further back. The crisis became virulent with the scandal surrounding the first female member of the federal government who, in a fateful phone call, informed her husband of the activities of the federal police about illegal business transactions in which he was involved. The inquiry which followed brought to light the extreme industry with which state security had been pursued: it found that 900 000 Swiss citizens had been spied on, that is almost a sixth of the population. The files, in parts amateurishly kept, were concerned with people's political affiliations and their contacts, especially with the 'red' East, which was seen during the Cold War as the evil empire. The only legitimate contacts with this evil realm were business transactions – this much had remained unchanged since the war.

In 1991, the *Fichen-Affäre*, this mountain of papers piled up to protect the country from its unreliable sons and daughters, was enough to spoil completely the party spirit among artists and intellectuals: they declared a cultural boycott. They no longer felt like celebrating Switzerland's birth 700 years earlier, sealed in the *Bundesbrief* between Uri, Schwyz and Unterwalden. An exception was Herbert Meier who wrote a long, patriotic play, *Mythenspiel*. However, the play, oozing with pathos and mythological clichés, left the valley of Schwyz, at the feet of the two *Mythen* (myths) – these mountains are really called that and they stand in the countryside, which has been dubbed Switzerland's cradle, like a warning finger – with a mountain of debt, rather than the expected patriotic enthusiasm and positive sense of national identity.

The nineteenth century had gone, irrevocably, and the great national festival Gottfried Keller had dreamt of in 1860 could not be celebrated with a delay of 100 years. Gottfried Keller was dreaming of this festival on the boat on the way to the inauguration of the Mythenstein (rock of the myths), a rock in front of the Rütli – the place where the old confederates allegedly swore their oath of union – which was dedicated to 'Tell's Bard', Friedrich Schiller, to keep alive the memory of the poet to whom Switzerland owes the myth of its origins.

The politician Andreas Iten observed in the upper house of parliament that the chance to contain the domestic policy crisis started by the *Fichen-Affäre* by means of celebrations in the year 1991 had been missed. That was ten days after a new debacle, when the Swiss voted against joining the EEA (European Economic Area) on 6 December 1992, a referendum which not only left the people and the government in opposed camps but also opened up a gulf between the German-speaking and the French-speaking parts of the country. A worried Andreas Iten asked in parliament what measures the Federal Council intended to adopt in order to re-create the lost sense of collective identity. He suggested that the commemoration year 1998 would present an ideal opportunity to do this. Andreas Iten's representations found a sympathetic ear: in October 1993 Federal Councillor Ruth Dreifuss agreed in her answer that remembrance of 1798 and 1848 – unlike that of 1291 – was all about the concrete analysis of history and not about historical legend.[1]

In those days, subjects like unclaimed assets, Nazi gold or, heaven forbid, less than impeccable conduct during the Second World War had not yet been discovered, but demands for historical research instead of repeated invocation of obsolete myths apply to this more recent era as much as they do to the memorable dates of 1798 and 1848. For the time being, no one can tell to what extent historical research can contribute to the Swiss identity the politicians so ardently wish for.

It will, no doubt, be some time before the results of the intensified historical analysis in the anniversary year 1998 find their way out of universities, newspapers and books into public awareness. The question we are concerned with here is the nature of the picture contemporary Swiss literature paints of its country of origin. Literature does not compete with politicians or historians in trying to question history or to resolve political crises. However, it does undoubtedly make its contribution towards questioning the country's image of itself. Whether literature can be used to strengthen a sense of collective identity or whether it is not more likely to help expose this identity as a myth is a question that will have to remain unanswered for the moment. At any rate, it is in the very nature of literature that it deals in myths, knowledge turned metaphor and materialised ideas. Maybe a country needs its myths in order to develop a collective identity. However, it would then be important not to mistake the myths for history, and to be clear about the difference between these two interpretations of the past which has formed the present and is still contributing to the future as a model.

On his journey across the Lake of Lucerne, which took him through a theatrical landscape – one that had been depicted by nineteenth-century painters as a heroic celebration of unworldly harmony – to the Mythenstein, the Schiller memorial, Gottfried Keller already knew in his time about the part played by mythology and legend in the history of Switzerland's origins. However, he also knew how to keep them in their place:

So wären wir füglich gezwungen, wenn keine Sage über die Entstehung oder Stiftung der Eidgenossenschaft vorhanden wäre, eine solche zu erfinden; da sie aber vorhanden ist, so wären wir Toren, wenn wir die Mühe nicht sparten. Mögen indessen die Gelehrten bei ihrer strengen Pflicht bleiben; wenn sie nur das mögliche Notwendige nicht absolut leugnen, um das Unmögliche an dessen Stelle zu setzen, nämlich die Entstehung aus nichts.[2]

Myths as an image of the possible – this is where the two approaches meet. The myth becomes a permanent reason to re-examine history and to use it to shed light on the myth. At the same time, the myth also challenges history to be faithful to the facts. Max Frisch demonstrated this in 1970 with his *Wilhelm Tell für die Schule* and in 1973 with his *Dienstbüchlein*, which is set in less obviously mythological–historical surroundings, yet still firmly rooted in the realm of the myth, where the Swiss army belongs as one of the institutions forming the Swiss collective identity. *Dienstbüchlein* is a more sober revision of *Blätter aus dem Brotsack* written by Max Frisch during his active service in the Second World War. Revision is a characteristic of the writing of history too: the fact that it is necessary is one of the reasons for Switzerland's current identity crisis. If history is not rewritten and revised constantly it turns into a myth. Adolf Muschg, in his latest book *O mein Heimatland*, which deals with Swiss politics and the author's personal conduct as a political animal, puts into words the categorical imperative for a realistic self-image:

> Die ganze Schweizergeschichte wird, im Licht eines Erkenntnisschocks, neu zu erzählen und dabei neu zu entdecken sein – zunächst die letzten unbekannt gewordenen 150 Jahre, deren Jubiläum jetzt zu feiern ist. Sie sind bisher im Schatten versunken, den die geistige Landesverteidigung nach hinten warf – oder vielmehr: sie sind vom Scheinwerferlicht ihrer Inszenierung ausgeblendet worden. Nun aber brauchen wir ein anderes Licht für unsere nächsten Stücke Wegs. In die Geschichte der andern einzutreten, wird von selbst dazu führen, daß wir die eigene Geschichte neu lesen. Viele ihrer Punkte werden erst einsehbar, wenn sich das Land bewegt. Die Schlüsselstellen sind da, nur fehlen uns einstweilen die Schlüssel dazu, und da, wo wir heute Licht haben, liegen sie nicht, sondern 'im Schatten der Vergangenheit' – bei weitem nicht nur denjenigen des Zweiten Weltkriegs.[3]

To reinterpret history: for this, at least, literature keeps our senses alert with its stories, which have a part in both, because they feed off them and they help create them, myths and history, in the form of which we can remember and retell reality.

Literature from Switzerland – we are here mainly concerned with the German-speaking part of the country – remains situated between myth and history, just as it remains engaged in antagonism between uneventfulness and historical events. This tension makes it productive, this tension between belonging and not belonging, which marks Switzerland's position in history. It finds expression in the ever-recurring relation of the self with the other in no other way than in the wish to take part, which clashes with the experience of unimportance.

In his narrative *Fremdes Land*, Jörg Steiner describes a scene at Geneva Airport: in a scuffle between members of the 'National Movement' and protesters, who want to stop the deportation of rejected asylum seekers back to Africa, a man is killed, Erich Jaag, 'der Sohn eines Halbbluts und selber ein Halbblut unter den Seßhaften. Der Name Jaag ist ein Name von Fahrenden, von Scherenschleifern, Hausierern, Pfannenflickern, Korbmachern und Färbern, und auch ein Name von Kundschaftern, Fährtenlegern und Fährtenlesern.'⁴ The last sentence of the narrative seems to want to take away all importance from what has been told. The narrator's voice belittles the event: 'Im Übrigen ist auf die Bedeutungslosigkeit des Vorfalls hinzuweisen; ein objektiver Beobachter würde sich hüten, ihn mit den großen Unruhen in der Welt zu vergleichen.'⁵ This is said as much ironically as thoughtfully. The sentence makes things smaller and deflects attention to what is big, it is an instance of ducking down to escape unscathed and free of guilt, it is an example of the modesty and self-effacement of which Robert Walser was a master. However, what is a stylistic device in literature turns into morally reprehensible behaviour if applied to history: literature and history become antagonists, the literary position exposes the historical one and makes it accessible to experience by creating an immediacy that is necessarily missing from any abstract treatment of history. The incident at Geneva Airport imbues Jaag's subjective story with every importance because it extinguishes his being and removes him from all worldly embroilment. It is an event in a small country, a subjective story situated on the edges of a place where there is no history. Jörg Steiner tells a story about the strange in the familiar by looking at his own country through foreign eyes. By breaking the perspective he makes the familiar, which has never been questioned, clear and questionable: 'wie soll einer, der nie eine Heimat gehabt hat, auf Heimat verzichten wollen?'⁶

It is only in the subjective mode that the big and the general can be grasped. This is what Peter Bichsel did in his *Kindergeschichten* and in the 'blackboard sentences' of his first prose piece *Eigentlich möchte Frau Blum den Milchmann kennenlernen*. The run-of-the-mill, the ordinary comes under the scrutiny of an eye that only sees the small, the particular, that does not see the big connections. However, it is in the gaps, in the border that has been left blank around the isolated details that the connections become apparent, that is where the 'big world' shows itself. In the same way, Robert Walser managed to extract meaning from the seemingly meaningless, to create literature out of uneventfulness.

Swiss uneventfulness? This is an identity-giving myth, born of the artist's suffering from emptiness and unproductivity, an important stylistic influence on literature from Switzerland – or is it a historical fact? Walser's *Prosastückli* were written not only in Berne and Biel, but also in Berlin and the precise vision of the ordinary was sharpened on the strange and on foreign views. Robert Walser may have experienced feelings similar to those experienced later by Thomas Hürlimann as he was telling stories of himself and his country in the bars of Berlin. It was only in the process of telling his stories that he realised that they were material for literature. All the more artistic for its unpretentiousness, 'Schweizerreise in einem Ford' from Thomas Hürlimann's first book *Die Tessinerin* provides insights into Swiss middle-class life from the distance of Berlin.

The familiar needs distance in order to become a fit subject for description. This is a key experience in Gertrud Leutenegger's writing. The first-person narrator's close-up view of a Valais observatory in *Kontinent* is seen in a new light through her observations of faraway China, which presents the visitor with experiences far removed from her own. In *Acheron* it is the tension between the familiar, in the guise of Ticino, and the foreign, represented by Japan, that provides the first-person narrator with bewildering and enlightening moments in equal measure. Beneath such openness towards the distant, however, there lies a closer viewpoint which is both an act of engaging with what is close and, at the same time, disconcerting distance. It is a viewpoint which creates a dialectical connection between the view from inside and that from outside, between the familiar and the foreign.

This model is already apparent in Gertrud Leutenegger's first book *Vorabend*. On the eve of a protest, the narrator walks through the streets of Zurich, along the route of the demonstration, in order to make sure of the place and to find clarity about herself, her own place in society and the world. 'So ganz richtig dabeizusein. Eine Demonstration! Denn nur Mitlaufen, das ist es nicht.'[7] It is all about making things one's own, about intensifying one's perception. The imminent event changes the way the world is seen, it makes it possible for familiar places, the self and its individual history, to be seen through a stranger's eyes. What moves society casts its shadow on the individual person, who, under the pressure of collective demands and the invitation to get involved, turns to his or her own history to separate the permanent from the unimportant ballast that should be shed. However, from time to time even the outdated has to be re-examined.

It is only through self-awareness that involvement becomes real, that the individual person does not move in a history-free vacuum, that they recognise their place in contemporary society defined through their relationships they have explored through self-examination.

With a consistency shared by few, Guido Bachmann in *Lebenslänglich. Eine Jugend* through this self-examination writes that being a fully fledged member of contemporary society depends on self-awareness. He makes Swiss history his own, personal history, when, after the first sentence 'Ich bin kein Schweizer',[8] he tells a piece of the social and political history of his own country in the story of a difficult father–son relationship.

Switzerland's history is a history of individual people: it is not just contemporary historiography that has moved away from the big sweeping movements of states – literature, which is not a suitable keeper of history anyway, has always written its own stories, which, even when they are based on historical reality, cannot be useful as a tool for the creation of an official image of Switzerland and, much less, as a reliable source for historical research. The relationship between literature and historical reality is complex and complicated and the creation of a national identity is not a task literature should be expected to accomplish. Not even critical questioning and deconstruction should be expected of it. Literature cannot be used as a tool, it is suitable neither for opposition nor for confirmation and affirmation (though it is naturally more sympathetic to the former): literature does not make states. On the contrary, as long as it maintains its standards as an art form it will always adopt the opposite position: writing means overstepping the boundaries of the conventional, it is Utopian enterprise and fulfilled yearning.

Literature does not take sides where it declares its intentions but in those cases where it concentrates on what is its own.

> Manchmal scheint auch mir, daß jedes Buch, so es sich nicht befaßt mit der Verhinderung des Kriegs, mit der Schaffung einer besseren Gesellschaft und so weiter, sinnlos ist, müßig, unverantwortlich, langweilig, nicht wert, daß man es liest, unstatthaft. Es ist nicht die Zeit für Ich-Geschichten. Und doch vollzieht sich das menschliche Leben oder verfehlt sich am einzelnen Ich, nirgends sonst.[9]

In this way, Max Frisch's Gantenbein explains people's right to their own, individual histories. It is always in the small, individual stories of little people that 'big' history is reflected, which goes beyond individual human beings. In *Albissers Grund*, published in 1974, Adolf Muschg explores the awakening of a political consciousness and the way back to anarchy through the story of an individual. Otto F. Walter relates the history of his country as the history of fathers in 1988 in *Zeit des Fasans*. Back in 1972, in *Die ersten Unruhen*, he deconstructed the individual by creating an objective view, by using fictitious and factual news he made the story tell itself. The anonymous narrative collective made the loss of the individual all the more poignant. Five years later, after the movement of 1968 had definitely foundered, the gap was filled in *Die Verwilderung* by two young lovers, who took on the part of the subject of history. Against society and pushed aside by it, Rob and Leni dare to make an idealistic attempt at living their vision of a liberated society. *Wie wird Beton zu Gras*, written in 1979, also tells the entirely private love story of a young woman and thus places the focus on the occupation of the building site for a nuclear plant in the story of an individual.

Is this the retreat from the political into the individual and the poetic? It is letting an individual loose in the events of history. It is history felt as hope and pain in one's own life and it is the opposite of retreat or running away. For Swiss artists, it is, as Paul Nizon postulates in 1970 in his *Diskurs in der Enge*, the only way out of their insignificance. 'In unserer Literatur reißen die Helden aus, um Leben unter die Füße zu bekommen – wie in Wirklichkeit die Schriftsteller ins Ausland fliehen, um erst einmal zu leben, um Stoffe zu erleben.'[10] Lack of subject matter was Nizon's diagnosis of contemporary narrative literature, and two types of escape from narrowness: running away and retreat into the spiritual world, with its inescapable end in madness.

However, I do not believe it was lack of subject matter that led to Robert Walser's madness – if it was madness and not rather a hermit's self-effacing retreat from the world. If anything, the reason for his madness was a lack of response to his writing and the impossibility of living off his poetry without betraying it or selling out.

Writers in Switzerland do not suffer from a lack of subject matter, a lack of topics. The question, though, is whether Switzerland is their subject. In 1965, Max Frisch left this question unanswered: 'Ist unser Land für seine Schriftsteller kein Gegenstand mehr? Und wenn es so sein sollte: Warum? Was heißt das in bezug auf das Land? Literatur ist eine Wünschelrute: wo sie nicht in Bewegung gerät, da ist keine Quelle. Ist das die Antwort? Ich weiß nicht.'[11] For Max Frisch himself, Switzerland was a lifelong subject. Again and again he proved wrong any suspicions that the source had dried up. Even his last work in 1989 was concerned with Switzerland. It examined the double myth of Switzerland and its army. Conservative politicians and army officers reacted to his 'Palaver' *Schweiz ohne Armee?* before the referendum on the abolition of the Swiss army with a renewed deepening of the gulf between the state and the arts. The text did not take sides, it was simply an invitation to critical discussion and the revision of preconceived opinions. Frisch himself, like the grandfather and active service veteran in this political dialogue with his grandson, re-examined his own positions and opinions, which he had written in 1940 during his active service in his *Blätter aus dem Brotsack* and revised and criticised in his *Dienstbüchlein* in 1974.

It was against the myths and against those well-meaning state representatives, who wanted to invite him to the celebrations of '700 years of confederation' in 1991, that Max Frisch was working on the concept of Switzerland, by which he meant something other than the 'verluderte Staat'[12] (run-down state), which had its citizens put under observation and registered their contacts in files. This was a scandal, which just would not fit in with the birthday party and which provoked the cultural boycott against the 'Schnüffelstaat' (snooping state): 'Der Mythos, den die Schweiz sich selber gibt, und die Tatsache, daß der Mythos keine Probleme löst; daher die Hysterie der Hilflosigkeit; jedes Problem, das wir selbst zu bewältigen haben, schickt den Begriff der Schweiz in die Reparatur. Hoffentlich gelingt sie.'[13] This was said in 1965, and it was reconfirmed three decades later. The myth-tinted image of a strong, neutral Switzerland was shaken, first by the discussion about Switzerland's role in Europe (provoked by the referendum in December 1992) and then by the controversy surrounding the attitude and actions of Switzerland spared in the Second World War, its business sense and its handling of the Nazi gold. Thus at last there was a subject for writers in Switzerland, or was their own country still not a topic?

In fact, it had been a topic for a long time and still remained one. Friedrich Dürrenmatt had already discussed the question of guilt and innocence in 1972 in a published fragment entitled *Dramaturgie der Schweiz*. Urs Faes with his 1989 novel *Sommerwende* is only one of many younger authors in Switzerland, who grapple with recent history, with the discrepancies between image and function, between the myth and Switzerland's conduct during the Second World War – not in pamphlets and essays, but in their literary works.

At least for the writers, for Switzerland's literature Peter Bichsel's comment in 1969 in *Des Schweizers Schweiz* is not valid: 'Unsere Vorstellung von unserem Land ist ein ausländisches Produkt. Wir leben in der Legende, die man um uns gemacht hat.'[14] The fact that Switzerland's own images, its own stories, which defended subjective truth against legend and made it possible for history to be experienced by the people, was not reflected at all (or at least not to a great extent) in the consciousness of the Swiss, is a different story. The way the Swiss deal with their country has always been marked by the belief in myths. There is nothing the inhabitants of this country hang on to more fiercely than their myths, which promise a permanent identity. Nothing is harder to get rid of than the ancient legends – which were not exclusively foreign imports like Schiller's *Wilhelm Tell*.

This also manifests itself in the debate around Ferdinand Hodler's large murals for the Swiss Museum in Zurich. The painting is a monumental depiction of the retreat from Marignano in 1515, which marked the end of Switzerland's involvement in power politics. This retreat is often seen as the starting point of Switzerland's uninvolved and therefore guilt-free neutrality, as if the reason for this move away from warfare had not been a defeat but rather the realisation of the importance of humanitarian values – values, moreover, whose meaning was not defined until much later. The fact that the traditional line of argumentation – the *Schlachtendiskurs*, which sees battles as identity-forming patriotic celebrations – was still alive long after Marignano, became clear in the artistic debate about Hodler's warriors, heroically emerging from the battle. Indeed, the Germanist Peter von Matt has shown that the critical patriotism, which has been a mark of Swiss literature in the second half of this century, has not managed to exorcise the myth connected with it: 'Max Frisch als Durchbruchs- und Leitfigur, dann die Diggelmann, Brodman, Hilty, Walter, Bichsel, Meienberg und ihre diversen Epigonen, sie haben aufgeräumt mit so zwielichtiger Art von nationaler Kommunikationsstiftung. Mythen waren das, und also wurde entmythisiert.'[15]

However, this 'de-mythologising' process did not go far enough; all it did was to reduce matters to

die Vorstellung von blauem Dunst [. . .], den man nur wegzublasen brauche. Unter dem Aspekt der 'Verhüllten Überlieferung' ist Mythos aber mehr: er ist nicht einfach Lüge, sondern eine Wahrheit in Lügengestalt, genauer noch: eine unerträgliche Wahrheit in Gestalt einer begeisternden Lüge. Die fraglos großartige Leistung des kritischen Patriotismus vom 'Stiller' bis zur 'Zeit des Fasans' fand ihre Grenze an dieser Vereinfachung. Man hat nur die Lüge denunziert; daß sie mit einer Wahrheit verwachsen war, hat man nicht gesehen.[16]

The *Schlachtendiskurs* mentioned above was a result of nineteenth-century historicism, it was an important factor contributing to the creation of a Swiss image and its influence can still be felt today. Below the surface, this *Schlachtendiskurs* also plays its part, either tacitly or reflected in irony, when contemporary Swiss authors confront their country and its history.

Peter von Matt makes the connection between the 'de-mythologising' process which is not far-reaching enough – what he calls 'critical patriotism', a product of the Cold War and its clear antagonisms – and the inadequate examination of the part Switzerland played in the Second World War:

Der kritische Patriotismus hat die Lüge des Schlachtendiskurses aufgedeckt, seiner Wahrheit war er nicht gewachsen. Er hat die Unmenschlichkeit des Hasses 'gegen die, welche nicht wir sind', ans Licht geholt, aber die Dimension der 'Erhebung über die Selbstsucht des Einzelnen', das Element einer gemeinsamen ethischen Verantwortlichkeit unterschlagen. Es ist zu vermuten, daß ohne die Mystifikationen des Schlachtendiskurses der indirekte Mord an den Juden an der verriegelten Schweizergrenze der vierziger Jahre nicht geschehen wäre, daß also das im Schlachtendiskurs freigesetzte Pathos der Gewalt auch diese Gewalt rechtfertigte. Aber das Potential an kollektivem Willen zu gegenseitiger Hilfe in der breiten Bevölkerung, das der Schweiz und vielen Flüchtlingen in der Schweiz Überleben half, nährte sich ebenfalls aus jenem komplexen Gefüge von Bildern und Zeichen. Insofern ist auch die Auseinandersetzung um die Landi 39 und die Geistige Landesverteidigung bis heute eindimensional und undialektisch geblieben.[17]

Unconsciously, the *Schlachtendiskurs* has been perpetuated in the latest myth, which has been further underpinned through onedimensional examination. This latest myth is the image of Switzerland as a self-sufficient hedgehog, which survived the Second World War by remaining strong and neutral. It is the fact that people are under the spell of myths, together with the hidden connection with the *Schlachtendiskurs*, which lies behind the indignation which still greets criticism and questions about the part played by neutral Switzerland during the war.

Wenn Auschwitz in der Schweiz liegt, wrote Adolf Muschg in 1997. With these words, he triggered a debate, not just among writers and intellectuals, about whether it is permissible to argue and make comparisons using an expression that has been misread and misunderstood as a metaphor.

Es ist wahr, und es ist ein Glück, daß die Schweiz den Krieg heil überlebt hat; es ist nicht wahr, daß sie gerechtfertigt daraus hervorgegangen ist. Und daß sie an diese Lüge ihre Identität gebunden hat, war nicht nur ein Unglück, es war eine Dummheit. Sie hat sich in einer Legende angesiedelt, mit der sie sich nicht nur von der Geschichte der anderen abhob, sondern auch von ihrer eigenen.[18]

The response to these words did not help to revise the outdated concept of Switzerland. On the contrary, the self-styled patriots were deeply offended and continued to cut themselves off from the outside world, claiming their country was a 'special case', a *Sonderfall*. However, Switzerland is not an island without a history. In literature, and long before the debate about Switzerland's role in the Second World War, this was made clear by the discussion initiated in 1992 by Dieter Bachmann in *Die Weltwoche*: 'Kann man noch Heimat sagen? 1991 hat das Zeitalter der Nachschweiz begonnen.'[19] His criticism of contemporary literature in Switzerland showed signs of being a new edition of Paul Nizon's *Diskurs in der Enge*. Bachmann demanded of Swiss literature 'the recognition of the global entanglement to which we are all subject'. Unfortunately, no books can be written about 'us all'. That is why his demands are in vain: 'What we really need are Swiss books that can mean the world.' However, they can only mean what is big if they contain what is small.

But what is small? It is the stories of individual people, the first-person narratives, in which life is realised, which turn the passage of time and the ways of the world into something that can be experienced. Only what comes from the experience of what is near can mean the world; what is far away needs the view of what is nearby. The experiences with one's own country have always been ambivalent in Switzerland. Ludwig Hohl was not the only one to complain: 'Das Land ist felsig, unfruchtbar, eng, ohne Meer.'[20] Max Frisch, too, was yearning for the sea, when, with a sigh, he noted in his diary in 1946:

> Wie klein unser Land ist. Unsere Sehnsucht nach Welt, unser Verlangen nach den großen und flachen Horizonten, nach Masten und Molen, nach Gras auf den Dünen, nach spiegelnden Grachten, nach Wolken über dem offenen Meer; unser Verlangen nach Wasser, das uns verbindet mit allen Küsten dieser Erde; unser Heimweh nach der Fremde.[21]

Restriction is both limitation and challenge. 'Hohe Horizonte', Peter Weber remarks in his first novel *Der Wettermacher* (1993), 'halten die Vorstellungskraft rundum im Zaum oder nötigen sie zu Höherem.'[22] Contrary to what Paul Nizon insinuates, these higher things cannot just be madness or 'Weltvernebelung' manifested in 'Weltentfremdung',[23] which seeks refuge in the mystical and the metaphysical. These higher things can be an intensity which concentrates on the small and ordinary, as Robert Walser has demonstrated. However, without the intensity of the view from outside the small remains ordinary and the ordinary small. That is what Ludwig Hohl meant when he wrote: 'Heimatliebe ist wahrscheinlich eine tiefstehende Form der Schöpferkraft; unmißverständlicher: desselben Elementes, das, wenn es seinen höheren Zustand erreicht, Schöpferkraft ist.'[24]

The high horizons become fatal when they block the view, either outwards or inwards, when the description of the particular does not go beyond reproduction. But where the description opens up, spreads its wings and soars high, there remains not a hint of national heritage. This is as true of Franz Böni and his stories about mountaineers and bone collectors as it is of Klaus Merz with his miniatures from the *Mittelland* and his short, dry sentences about loss and grief. It is true of the messages from ordinary life, which Margrit Baur or Helen Meier record in their narratives. It is true of Gerhard Meier's conversations between the old comrades Baur and Bindschädler in his trilogy *Toteninsel* (1979), *Borodino* (1982) and *Die Ballade vom Schneien* (1985).

If one looks at the work of Swiss women writers, one encounters a different way in which literature can only capture the big things, the things that move the world, by creating the small. One finds a different way of making the particular, the individual, accessible to the many. Until 1971, Swiss politics remained the domain of men; it was only after several attempts that Swiss men finally voted in favour of giving women the right to vote. For this, many metaphors can be found in narratives written by women, even though the parallels are never drawn explicitly: there are girls, for example in Theres Roth-Hunkeler's *Gehschule*, who are looking for their own place, their own language in a world dominated by fathers and men in general. These adolescent girls and young women, who can also be found in the works of Margrit Schriber, Mariella Mehr, Helen Meier, Christina Viragh, and more recently, those of Zoë Jenny and Ruth Schweikert, are not looking to their mothers to find a role model, but to find a feminine world. They rebel against a female role model dictated to them by men. The search for the mother, as well as her rejection, the resistance to traditional values and traditional ways of life, manifest themselves in the acquisition of a language and an existence, as literary critic Beatrice von Matt has put it.[25] Identity turns into a process of demarcation, the aim of which is not generality but individuality, self-sufficiency, no matter how painful it is to attain. This is indeed something totally different from the male *Schlachtendiskurs* – this is precisely dialectical confrontation that goes beyond binary thinking, that aims for demarcation and at the same time maintains contacts across the boundaries. This ambivalent process is shown particularly clearly by Christina Viragh in her third novel *Mutters Buch*, published in 1997. Although told differently, with a different starting point, Zoë Jenny's book of the same year, *Das Blütenstaubzimmer*, too, is a story of a search for identity with two faces, which looks for dependencies and independence in the same dialectical process, overthrows and overcomes them. It is the story of the creation of an image of the self that does not accept or allow relationships unquestioningly, but purifies them and accepts and forms them as a necessary part of its own identity.

As in these women's stories of detachment and demarcation, which seek dialogue, Switzerland does not have to be the explicit subject of such literary investigations that connect the outer with the inner. It is not even necessary that these works are set within the Swiss borders, as for example *In Trubschachen*, E. Y. Meyer's disturbing account of the modern world which is set in the Emmental. Even a novel like Rudolf Bussmann's *Die Rückseite des Lichts*, with its setting outside the real world, speaks in every line of Swiss reality. It speaks of economic power and bureaucracy, of the relegation of art into darkness, without being set in an identifiable place.

These are Swiss topics and at the same time they are not. Captured in the local and the accessible, they are the reflections of global processes, thinking and actions typical of their time, without there having to be any talk of globalisation. Sexuality and violence, as Hansjörg Schertenleib confronts them in his novel *Das Zimmer der Signora*, or the delicate relationship between joy and pain, as Christoph Geiser deals with them in his novels, these are subjects that cannot be set within the borders of one single small country.

In view of the fact that books like these exist, even books like those of Marcel Konrad, who deals with the same subjects in a rural setting, it is futile to search for the specifically Swiss in contemporary Swiss literature. This has less to do with the recognition of global connections, and is more the expression of a badly conceived question. The typically Swiss might be something that is found in a purely linguistic analysis of texts from Switzerland, which concentrates on semantic and grammatical peculiarities. However, even there things are no longer that simple, since the sons and daughters of foreigners who came to Switzerland in search of jobs started enriching Swiss literature with their own voices. In their writing, the strangeness of the language, which is felt by most Swiss authors, manifests itself doubly. To the second generation, the written 'high' language is a foreign language in two respects: it is different from their mother tongue and it is different from the dialect of their country of residence. Authors like Francesco Micieli, Franco Supino, Dante Andrea Franzetti or Perikles Monioudis write detached from their linguistic origins, their own subjects are described in a sensitised, more attentively used language.

These are refractions and alienations that do not hinder literature, but rather have a creative effect, because in this way, rules and conventions lose their predetermining power. Ludwig Hohl puts homelessness, disturbed certainties in life as well as language, above any unreflected sense of belonging: 'Alle großen geistigen Leistungen sind aus der Heimatlosigkeit entstanden.'[26]

Homelessness allows a view from outside of things that are familiar to others with less sensitive perception. In Switzerland – apart from the second generation of worker immigrants – it is women like Erica Pedretti, Hanna Johansen and Christina Viragh who stand for this kind of view. In *Unstete Leute, Rufe von jenseits des Hügels* and in *Mutters Buch*, Christina Viragh, who was born in Hungary and who emigrated to Switzerland at the age of seven, links the question of the formation of certainties, out of which grows a sense of belonging and home, to the search for memories – once more, the experience of a century, marked by migration and emigration, is reflected in a search for identity in the uncertain nature of an individual existence.

Such sensitivity for what cannot be taken for granted in references that can be shared and communicated means that authors like Nicole Müller and Andrea Simmen use language as a medium for description only with reservations. Behind the images there is a constant questioning voice which cannot be ignored and is also present in Hermann Burger's work. It is a sceptical alertness which, wide awake, watches language.

Taking words literally, listening to their meaning with never-tiring alertness, these are marks of Zsusanna Gahse's *Kellnerroman*, which she wrote in Switzerland and also set in the Swiss countryside. Is this literature from Switzerland? This author, too, is homeless, does not have a home country. Born in Hungary, she emigrated via Austria to

Germany and chose Switzerland as her place for writing. The way she observes the gestures, attentively listens to the language, is different, foreign, in a way that makes others understand what is familiar to them, turning what has been taken for granted into something unusual, something to be questioned. Friederike Kretzen, who has been living and working in Basle for years, does something similar in her work.

Of course, such alienation is not suitable for the creation of myths; it undermines any attempt to live with simple signs and images, described as trivial myths by Urs Widmer: 'Unsere Köpfe sind voll mit Heldenbildern, Vorstellungen, Dingen, die ganz selbstverständlich so sind, wie sie sind, obwohl sie möglicherweise ganz anders sind, mit Personen, Gegenständen und Ereignissen, die nicht nur sind, sondern für uns auch etwas bedeuten.'[27] Images and ideas that have been frozen into trivial myths have no liberating effect. No Utopian power would allow them to fulfil their potential for change, their only aim is to persist and confirm the status quo:

(Triviale) Mythen sind starre, auf weniges reduzierte Abziehbilder von dem, was wir Wirklichkeit nennen. Der (triviale) Mythos ist eindimensional und unreflektiert, er zeigt nur seine schöne Oberfläche. Er ist statisch, er ist unpolitisch, er gilt jetzt, seine historische Entwicklung (das, was dahinter steckt) kümmert mich nicht. Er will von Veränderungen nichts wissen, er hält am Status quo fest. Er ist reaktionär, und das ist das einzige, was an ihm irgendwie politisch aussieht.[28]

Trivial myths play with emotions, but what they will not allow is fear and insecurity. These beautiful and sad carbon copies of reality gather up individual yearnings into one single, common view; they replace the fear of the individual with the becalmed superficial image of the many.

Urs Widmer does not demolish these myths, he plays with them, he demonstrates how available they are, how they can be used as tools and thus he immunises his readers against their temptations. This is shown by his play about the Swiss ambassador in Berlin during the Second World War, *Frölicher – ein Fest* (1991) and no less by *Jeanmaire. Ein Stück Schweiz* (1992), his play about a high-ranking officer in the Swiss army, accused of treason. His attack is not aimed at the characters and the myths whose representatives they have become, but at the observer who contents himself with a view of the surface, who sticks with the real and blots out the unreal, the fantastic and the unlikely.

Both *Frölicher* and *Jeanmaire* are plays about history, the country and its history are explicitly their subject matter. However, the point here is not to find the truth, what really happened. For Urs Widmer irreverently plays with the historical characters, even when they are called Hitler and Eva Braun; he shows that they have long ago turned into trivial myths, into pictures of a collective imagination which are based on fantasy as much as on reality. To see both, to mistrust both and to see through trivial myths as the intellectual crutches they are is the moral of these plays.

Thomas Hürlimann, on the other hand, handles the historical character of the Swiss ambassador in Berlin completely differently in his play *Der Gesandte* (1991). He is interested in the fulfilment of duty and the gratitude of the fatherland. He shows no myths, no projections of the popular interpretations of history turned into a rigid cardboard copy of reality. Similarly, in *Der große Kater* (1998) he portrays the President of the Confederation – a picture puzzle of his father, who was the head of the Swiss Home Office from 1974 to 1982 and the President of the Confederation in 1974, the year in which the novel is set – as the individual human being behind his political function. It is not the aim of the novel to portray an episode of Switzerland's history, but to portray a powerful person operating in this episode. Thus the focus of the book is not on the external events, which have been fictionalised, but on the individual story of the protagonist, his path through life from the days of his child-hood, via monastery school, to his political office. The machinations and secret mechanisms at work in the centre of power are not por-trayed as the automatic workings of an anonymous machine, but as the concrete actions of individuals, who are intimately connected with each other. Power becomes visible as the consequence of indi-vidual actions – politics becomes ethically and morally responsible. Written with knowledge of the inner circles of power, this is an act of de-mythologising, not of a traditional myth this time, but of a more recent, trivialised myth, which can easily be mistaken for a cliché. Still, even to this trivial myth, tradition and historical derivation make their contribution. By making the explicitly individual view of history his literary subject, Thomas Hürlimann shows that history makes suitable literary subject matter, but, at the same time, he makes it clear that his way of handling history is different from that of professional historians, which builds on historical sources. In the same way, Urs Widmer, in his latest novel *Im Kongo* (1996), refutes the trivial myth of the uneventfulness of recent Swiss history with an individual and at the same time historical story. The father of the first-person narrator proves to be deeply entangled in the history of the Second World War. Contrary to what his son thinks, he does have an interesting, fateful, past – he was the Swiss secret service agent who was responsible for the direct line to Hitler's headquarters. Widmer uses elements of the real story of Emil Häberli, public prosecutor in Basle, to whose memory he dedicated the book, but he is not predominantly concerned with factual history. He simply uses it to refute a trivial myth: he demolishes the myth of complete neutrality, of Switzerland's non-involvement during the war. The fact that, in the Congo, white people who emphatically take part in the rites of the natives turn black, is a poignant metaphor for the other side of the myth of uneventfulness, which has been exposed as a lie. It is a metaphor for the fact that, in guilty times, no one escapes guilt.

This book shows Urs Widmer at the height of historical confrontation and, at the same time, at the height of his literary work, which holds up to the power of reality the strength of the fantastic, which holds up poetry to facts and which dares to meet horror with beauty. This is not possible in any other way than by making conscious the feelings of alienation and facing up to them, rather than remaining silent and covering them up. Urs Widmer does not accept the trivial myths, nor does he show blind trust in the factual. Switzerland and its history provide him with subject matter, but not a straitjacket. He does not treat historical facts differently from the way in which he treats the icons and legends of trivial myths – they are ready grist to his mill. That does not mean that a falsification of history has to result. This is about the gap between the real and the unreal, about the truth that cannot be had, that can only be sought. And it is about emotions which are needed to make history accessible, to bring it into the present.

The Manichean models have proved unsuitable, the concepts lose their sharp contours, as the borders become more and more permeable. Homelessness no longer stands in sharp contrast to home, which perhaps is nothing more than a place where someone has been for some time, a place they know well: 'Ich bin hier geboren. Ich bin hier aufgewachsen. Ich verstehe die Sprache dieser Gegend. Ich weiß, was ein Männerchor ist, was eine Dorfmusik ist, ein Familienabend einer Partei. Nur hier kann ich mit Sicherheit Schüchterne von Weltgewandten unterscheiden.'[29] Thus Peter Bichsel captures that which makes what is close familiar, what makes foreign places a place of open signs, whose meaning cannot always be divined. However, this uncertainty, this openness liberates, it ensures that perception does not become blunted, that it is possible to see new things.

It is the women among Switzerland's writers who are more inclined to allow this uncertainty of perception, who admit the strange into their language and their subject matter. The question as to what is certain and binding, the historical subjects, the questions of national identity and the creation of myths – things connected with the fatherland and the army, be they described in heroic terms or not – this is the subject matter of the men. In his novels, Otto Marchi, who wrote *Eine Schweizergeschichte für Ketzer*, concerns himself again and again with the question of truth, of the reliability of sources and the problem, not only epistemological, of objective and subjective factuality. This is the consistent theme that leads to questioning the identity of a country, which recognises its own image not in reality but in myths.

The fact that there is national service for men only partially explains why it is they who are more likely to write heroic stories, *Heldengeschichten*, and who engage in the *Schlachtendiskurs* which provided a platform for Meinrad Inglin's *Schweizerspiegel* in the 1930s, in which he reflects the image Switzerland painted of itself in the First World War, and which also provided Hermann Burger with a basis for his course in navigation through fog and life in his first novel *Schilten* (1977). This covert, insufficiently understood *Schlachtendiskurs* has been turned into an identity-sustaining metaphor in the Swiss army. It remains a metaphor, beyond all the real connections that exist between the army, politics and the economy. 'Die Schweiz ist zuerst einmal eine Armee und dann erst eine Demokratie.'[30] These are the words of Reto Hänny who, in *Zürich, Anfang September*, described another of the state's structural powers, the police, with the painfully accurate view of a victim of such power, as someone involved in the protests of a restless Zurich youth in 1980. This view does not need the strange or the foreign to render the unusual recognisable. This view can no longer simply be ascribed to male or female perception. What is important is the suffering, not the inflicting of power, and in the suffering, the subsequent recording of the suffering, the reflection of the process of becoming a stranger in one's own body. It is a process of turning into a collective entity, without losing oneself, it is an ambivalence between closeness and strangeness: 'mit Sprachen, in Wut und Spiel mit Fantasie enge Grenzen überwindend auf vielfältigsten Ebenen sich verflechtend und durchdringend, vom Körper getragen, aber nicht alleingelassen.'[31] To break the male view of male myths was Otto F. Walter's big project in his novel *Zeit des Fasans*. He only succeeded in part and what he attempted was achieved in a different way by Erica Pedretti with her novel *Engste Heimat*. Her subject matter, beyond the topic of Switzerland spared by war, set in the centre of the event and not the uneventfulness, concentrates on the aesthetically minimal distance of close-up suffering and distanced observation, connecting a not too distant 'there' with a contemporary 'here'. Perception and expression become an existential process of securing a self which creates reality and its place in it only by means of its own story: 'Als wäre alles, was nicht auszusprechen, nicht aufzuzeichnen, darzustellen gelingt, nie gewesen, und wäre nicht nur für ihn, Gregor, sondern auch für mich und alle Welt verloren.'[32]

We have asked how a national myth is created. A rhetorical question, there is no doubt about that. Literature is not a suitable instrument for such a purpose; nor could anyone expect it to solve a domestic policy crisis. Switzerland's identity crisis will last – a not unexpected dilemma for a country without a vision, a country whose state Friedrich Dürrenmatt lamented on 22 November 1990, shortly before his death, in a speech in honour of Vaclav Havel, when he described Switzerland as grotesque. He described it as a prison, in which the prisoners are their own warders and therefore paradoxically free. It was in a prison, too, that Max Frisch had his protagonist in *Stiller* voice his criticism of Switzerland – ingeniously reflected in personal identity crisis. For Stiller does not want to be Stiller, he claims to be an American called Jim White. However, his passport is forged and when he crosses the Swiss border in Basle he is immediately arrested. The reluctant Stiller resists the identity imposed on him by creating the adventurous White-identity, an alternative design not only against bourgeois narrowness, which Stiller had fled, but also one against the Swiss, who have turned the momentous year 1848 into a myth and a memorial, which has no effect on, nor meaning for, the present and the future. Gottfried Keller said the legend of William Tell would have had to be invented if Schiller had not done so. But even he, the revolutionary of 1848 and guerrilla in the *Freischaren* skirmishes before the federal state was established, expressed his disappointment about betrayed ideals and lost Utopia in his late novel *Martin Salander*: for him Switzerland had declined into a marriage of convenience of preachers of progress, with power and wealth its only objectives. In his play *Das Lied der Heimat*, first performed in the spring of 1998 in Zurich, Thomas Hürlimann has a depressed Gottfried Keller flee the 'Festschwindel' around his 70th birthday and escape to Seelisberg, high above the Lake of Lucerne, where, as a (as yet unrecognised) grumpy guest, he complains about the 'verluderte Staat' (Max Frisch's words):

Zum Kotzen! Und eins kann ich Ihnen sagen, Herr Ober: Ich denke nicht daran, von den dummen Lobsprüchen dieser Herren überfallen zu werden. Deshalb bin ich hierhergeflüchtet. Ich wollte keine Lobhudeleien, keine Reden, keine verlogenen Hurras. Zerreißen Sie das Telegramm! Der Staat, den wir gemeint haben, wir 48er, ist liberal. Ist revolutionär. Laßt jeden denken und sagen und schreiben, was er will! Ist das klar? Wir sind nicht auf die Barrikaden geklettert und, was noch schwieriger war, durch die Bureaus und Schreibstuben gegangen, um am Schluß unseres Lebens von Polizei-Spitzeln verfolgt zu werden. Unser Ziel war die Freiheit, Herr Ober. Ein liberaler Staat. Eine echte Demokratie. Und was ist aus unseren Idealen geworden? Eine Festhütte! Jeder Anlaß zum Feier, und ist es ein alter Schreibknecht, wird am Schopf gepackt, aus seiner Ruhe gelupft und mit verlogenem Eifer angebetet! Höhenfeuer, wohin man blickt! Lächerlich, Herr Ober, ein Festschwindel! In den Kontoren lagern Raubgelder, Ferkelkrösusse und Schlauköpfe prellen das Volk um Kapital und Zinsen, und wiewohl alle tun, als würden sie die Posten von Soll und Haben hübsch verbuchen, als seien Aktien auf Treu und Glauben erworben, ist auch das ein Schwindel. Festschwindel und Kapital-

schwindel! Ha, und erst die Politik! Was wahre Staats- und Gesell-
schaftsfreunde geschaffen haben, ist von Ober-, Mittel- und
Unterstrebern längst verbogen worden, die Phantasie zerfloß in
Trübseligkeit, die Herren Revolutionäre grüßen als Sonntagsspa-
ziergänger, und die Herren Volksvertreter schachern im Halb-
dunkel von Bierstuben um Ämtlein und Sitzungsgelder.[33]

This sounds utterly contemporary, and yet those are not words put
into Keller's mouth, but a quotation from his writings.

Switzerland does not need a new myth, it does not even need to
turn into a nation – these myths of the nineteenth century have
reached the end of their useful lives just as the world view of the
Cold War has collapsed. As a state, Switzerland should stay a confederation of the different, and as such it will have to keep re-examining
its identity. With its metaphors and sketches, literature can help the
process, not because it can be used as a tool for political purposes,
but because it reflects politics and uses the myths against history.
Thus it constantly reinvents the past and revitalises the moribund.
For even when literature is concerned with history, it still keeps an
eye on the other; it does not go for the real but for the fantastic, that
which can be changed first. It takes history as a given and still rebels
against the factual. It does not content itself with just one image of
the past, that one-dimensionality which characterises every trivial
and unquestioned myth.

Making history feel real, making the facts come to life, that is what
literature is about: it is about the transformation of history, for the
sake of the present and the future. This cannot be done any other
way than by crossing the boundaries of the factual and the real
towards the unreal and the fantastic. From that journey, all art
receives its Utopian and transforming power: one day, the unreal,
unlike the real, will have an effect that crosses the gulf of estrange-
ment into a reality which is realistic because it is what has been
agreed upon. This is why literature engages with reality and chooses,
for example, a country and its history as its subject.

Translated by Corinne Iten

Notes

1. 'Jubiläen der Schweizer Geschichte 1798–1848–1998'. *Zeitschrift des Schweizerischen Bundesarchivs. Studien und Quellen*, 24 (Berne, Stuttgart, Vienna, 1998), pp. 272ff.
2. Thomas Bäning *et al.* (eds), *Gottfried Keller. Sämtliche Werke in sieben Bänden*, vol. 7, *Aufsätze, Dramen, Tagebücher* (Frankfurt am Main, 1996), p. 166.
3. Adolf Muschg, *O mein Heimatland. 150 Versuche mit dem berühmten Schweizer Echo* (Frankfurt am Main, 1998), pp. 215f.
4. Jörg Steiner, *Fremdes Land* (Frankfurt am Main, 1989), p. 9.
5. Ibid., p. 113.
6. Ibid., p. 97.
7. Gertrud Leutenegger, *Vorabend* (Frankfurt am Main/Zurich, 1975), p. 7.
8. Guido Bachmann, *Lebenslänglich. Eine Jugend* (Basle, 1997), p. 9.
9. Max Frisch, *Mein Name sei Gantenbein*, in: Hans Mayer and Walter Schmitz (eds), *Gesammelte Werke in zeitlicher Folge*, vol. V (Frankfurt am Main, 1976), p. 68.
10. Paul Nizon, *Diskurs in der Enge* (Frankfurt am Main, 1990), p. 169.
11. Max Frisch, 'Unbewältigte schweizerische Vergangenheit?', in: Max Frisch, *Schweiz als Heimat?* (Frankfurt am Main, 1990), pp. 217f.
12. Max Frisch, 12 March 1991, letter to Marco Solari, du, *Die Zeitschrift der Kultur*, 12 (1991), 104.
13. Max Frisch, 'Überfremdung I', in: Max Frisch, *Schweiz als Heimat?*, p. 221.
14. Peter Bichsel, *Des Schweizers Schweiz* (Zurich, 1969), p. 15.
15. Peter von Matt, 'Die Gewalt. Der Schlachtendiskurs. Das Fest', in: Jürg Huber and Martin Heller (eds), *Konturen des Unentschiedenen. Interventionen 6* (Basle, Frankfurt am Main, 1997), p. 104.
16. Ibid., p. 104.
17. Ibid., pp. 104f.
18. Adolf Muschg, *Wenn Auschwitz in der Schweiz liegt* (Frankfurt am Main, 1997), pp. 12f.
19. Dieter Bachmann, 'Kann man noch Heimat sagen?', *Die Weltwoche*, 30 April 1992, pp. 63f.
20. Ludwig Hohl, *Die Notizen oder Von der unvoreiligen Versöhnung* (Frankfurt am Main, 1981), p. 508.
21. Max Frisch, *Tagebuch 1946–1949. Gesammelte Werke*, vol. II, p. 364.
22. Peter Weber, *Der Wettermacher* (Frankfurt am Main, 1993), p. 77.
23. Nizon, *Diskurs in der Enge*, p. 177.
24. Ludwig Hohl, *Von den hereinbrechenden Rändern. Nachnotizen* (Frankfurt am Main, 1986), pp. 155f.
25. Beatrice von Matt, 'Die Sprache der Mutter, das Heimweh der Töchter. Kindheitsrecherchen von Autorinnen aus der deutschsprachigen Schweiz', *Neue Zürcher Zeitung*, 12/13 September 1998, p. 67.
26. Hohl, *Von den hereinbrechenden Rändern*, p. 85.
27. Urs Widmer, 'Über (triviale) Mythen', in: Urs Widmer, *Das Normale und die Sehnsucht. Essays und Geschichten* (Zurich, 1972), p. 21.
28. Ibid., p. 22.

29. Bichsel, *Des Schweizers Schweiz*, p. 21.
30. Reto Hänny, *Am Boden des Kopfes. Verwirrungen eines Mitteleuropäers in Mitteleuropa* (Frankfurt am Main, 1991), p. 227.
31. Reto Hänny, *Zürich, Anfang September* (Frankfurt am Main, 1981), p. 132.
32. Erica Pedretti, *Engste Heimat* (Frankfurt am Main, 1995), p. 85.
33. Thomas Hürlimann, *Das Lied der Heimat* (Zurich, 1998), pp. 22ff.

Part II

4

Reforming the Swiss Federal Constitution: an International Lawyer's Perspective

Thomas Cottier

Introduction

Celebrations of the 150th birthday of the Swiss Federal Constitution and the present constitutional debate in Switzerland do not attract much attention abroad. Geographically, Switzerland is a small country of a mere 7 million inhabitants, neutral, not a member of the European Union and leading what many consider to be a boring public life. It seems to live somewhat on its own, in splendid isolation. It has a regime of arcane federalism and of direct democracy, all located in the middle of Western European nation states and a white spot on the map of the European Union. Not astonishingly, Switzerland hardly appears to be the source of constitutional inspiration and a model for running a modern society and nation at the beginning of the twenty-first century. If at all, Europeans were and are still looking to the traditions of the United States' Constitution, certainly not to the small odd man out in their own midst. This benevolent ignorance is partly due to pride and prejudice, nurtured by incremental and often unfavourable press coverage of the country. Much of the latter is due to ignorance and insufficient exposure to history, the traditions, the structure and problems of Switzerland. But most of it is due to the country's chosen path of political non-alliance and independence as defined by former generations, and the fate of not having shared the devastating experiences of war on the continent in the last century.

I am thus grateful to have the opportunity to assist in bringing about a somewhat different perception of Switzerland and the role its constitutional experience and problems may provide for the building of Europe in the twenty-first century. In the context of building a federal and decentralised Europe, recent years have brought enhanced attention to the Swiss constitutional experience of bringing together a society of different cultures over the last 150 years.[1] In particular, instruments of direct democracy beyond voluntary plebiscites are increasingly considered an interesting approach to bringing about stability and legitimacy of the law (even though a critical observer suggests that the idea of being a model for Europe is perhaps an idea dreamed up by the Swiss).[2] Historically, Switzerland was the first modern European republic. In 1848, when it emerged in the aftermath of the Napoleonic Wars, restoration and the years of liberal revolutions, it was surrounded by conservative monarchies and nations. The Constitution was largely modelled on the United States Constitution of 1776 to which French ideas of direct democracy were added later in order to rebalance powers among the different regions. It provided the foundation for the first multicultural federation in Western Europe, linking Alemannic, French, Italian and Raeto-Roman cultures. It provided the foundation for building a liberal single market throughout the country; and it provided the basis, later on, for building the welfare state and cohesion among the different parts of the country. Finally, it created the conditions for an open and prosperous economy. I just note in passing that for many years, Switzerland has been the second largest trading partner of the EU in terms of imports from the Community, and the third largest, following the United States and Japan, in terms of exports to the EU,[3] trade in services not being included in these figures. Trade flows of the EU with contemporary Switzerland are larger than to all of the middle and eastern European countries put together. And, as a future member of the EU, net contributions will amount to some 3.5–4 billion SF (2.2–2.4 euro).[4] This will bring Switzerland into the range of the second or third largest net contributor, following Germany and perhaps the Netherlands.[5]

In light of the country's history, integrationist and economic success, it might therefore be of some interest to look into the life and problems of that boring place. This essay will not explain the political system and how it operates.[6] I should like to focus rather on constitutional reform. And I shall do this from my perspective as an international lawyer by looking at conditions and requirements to which national constitutions in the twenty-first century need to focus and respond. This, in many ways, is a somewhat unusual, but in my view necessary, perspective, since constitutional law and lawyers still largely tend to ignore the challenges of regional and global legal integration in reshaping national constitutions.

This perspective may also be of some comparative interest. Comparable, if not similar issues arise with all federal constitutions in Europe, and indeed, around the world. Moreover, the experiences and issues in Switzerland may be of some assistance in shaping the future of the emerging European constitutional order which, in the form of the Maastricht and Amsterdam treaties, has come a long way since the days of the founding fathers in the 1950s. It amounts, in substantive terms, to constitutional federal structures, granting, limiting and balancing democratic powers in a multicultural setting. In fact, teaching European law in Switzerland amounts very much to a comparative exercise as we find a large number of parallels in the evolution and the features of the two constitutions.

The reform process of the Swiss Constitution

Wolf Linder likes to describe Switzerland as having the most stable government and the most unstable Constitution.[7] Indeed, since the last comprehensive overhaul in 1974, it has been amended more than 130 times – much more than, for example the US Constitution. Key areas such as the fiscal powers are deliberately put in the form of transitory provisions, apt to amendment as such needs occur. A closer look, however, reveals that the written Constitution has not changed in its fundamental structures of government: federalism, neutrality, direct democracy, even power-sharing among main political parties. Most of the changes are due to the fact that the federal Constitution – much like the EC treaty and unlike the US Constitution – operates on a principle of enumerated powers enshrined in Article 3 of the Federal Constitution. It operates on the historical assumption that the 26 cantons are sovereign, and thus all federal tasks need to be explicitly ascribed to, and defined in, the Constitution. Moreover, Article 123 of the Federal Constitution prescribes for reasons of federal balance that such allocations need a double majority both of the overall participating Swiss voters and, in addition, of the cantons. And this explains why – unlike the EU and the US – doctrines of implied powers never found a fruitful soil in Switzerland, except for fundamental rights where the Supreme Court, during an important period in the 1970s, recognised a number of unwritten constitutional rights,[8] not explicitly mentioned in the Federal Constitution. This is so because the main function of the Federal Constitution was at the time – and not unlike the Treaty of Rome – to bring about an internal market, but not to protect all the liberties of the citizens. This was mainly assigned to the constitutions of the cantons and later on, to the Swiss Supreme Court.

It is hardly astonishing that the Constitution – very much an instrument of government and politics – these days looks like a tired old warhorse of the daily political process, bruised and not exactly elegant in shape. Without knowledge of Latin numbering – *bis, ter, quater* up to *septies* or *octies* – you cannot follow the text. More seriously, however, it was felt in the 1960s that the structure of government – designed in the eighteenth century – was no longer apt for coping with the modern state, and efforts to bring about a more efficient and also a more central allocation of powers were undertaken. These efforts at bringing about substantive changes resulted in substantial reports of constitutional commissions in 1973, and in a draft proposal submitted in 1977. The latter suggested, in the wake of 1968, a number of reforms, in particular in the allocation of powers between the cantons and the federal government, and put more faith in central government and state activities than before.[9] Parliament, however, failed to follow suit, and the project was buried. There was no majority, let alone a consensus that an overhaul was necessary. These attitudes reflect basic Swiss qualities and federalism: policy and politics in this country are inherently pragmatic, piecemeal and bottom up; quite like in England, I dare say (except for federalism, which, on the continent, and unlike in Anglo-American terminology, stands for the proposition of decentralisation). Swiss constitutional law is not the place of grand political designs. Periods marked by grand concepts of political planning did not achieve much.

Still, the idea of constitutional reform did not die away. A number of cantons managed to update and facelift their constitutions (some with substantial changes and innovations),[10] and similar efforts were held to be useful enough by the government and constitutional lawyers to be undertaken on the federal level. In 1987, parliament decided to take a low-key approach and requested the government to submit a draft which would reflect, in a descriptive manner, written and unwritten constitutional law. To some extent, it is like asking you to write down a British Constitution without changing it at the same time. The limits of four official languages and linguistics, of course, inherently bring about changes in the law as it is written down. But overall, the present project of 1996, currently under discussion in parliament, reflects the Swiss political and constitutional system as it emerged over time. Overall, with exceptions, the glossators did a wonderful job. We are quite reminded of their early brethren in the eleventh and twelfth centuries codifying Roman law, or later on, of the process of codification of civil law in the eighteenth and nineteenth centuries when written and centralised law gradually replaced customary law in order to establish liberal societies in the Napoleonic age and afterwards. The government faithfully stuck to the parameters set forth by parliament in 1987, and parliament itself has not introduced important changes, perhaps with the exception of fundamental rights where formulations adopted may not remain without impact on the way these rights have been construed, so far, by the Supreme Court.[11] In particular, minimal and justiciable social rights, still frail in the Court's jurisprudence, are politically reinforced. Another reinforcement relates to the role of the cantons in foreign affairs (Art. 50 of the Draft Constitution, hereafter DC). In response to efforts and voices seeking further reform, the government, in addition, proposes a number of packages and building blocks for reform later on, once the new codification has been adopted. Such reforms have been prepared in the fields of direct democracy (Project B)[12] and the judicial system (Project C). In the latter, parliament will be asked to submit constitutional judicial review of federal statutes which as of today have been excluded except where the matter touched upon rights guaranteed by the European Convention on Human Rights. Later on, additional reforms of the governmental system may be introduced on the basis of the same philosophy.[13] All the changes proposed in additional projects are highly controversial, and are not likely to see the light of day in coming years. It is possible that the project, as amended by parliament, will remain limited to the *mise à jour* (*Nachführung*) and submitted to the people and the cantons for double majority voting possibly in the year 1999 or 2000. (In fact, the project was accepted by a narrow majority in spring 1999.)

The dilemmas of the project

The academic observer faces a difficult dilemma with the 1996 project. On the one hand, the overall draft is a piece of excellent legal craftsmanship. The structure, chapters and formulation are mostly well and carefully chosen, and there is little doubt that the new dress of the Swiss Constitution, even after being amended by parliament, will ably reflect and update contemporary constitutional law. Citizens will have a better view of their rights, albeit, of course, the scope of these rights continues to be further defined in case law. The need to respond to new challenges by means of unwritten law will remain unaltered even under an expanded catalogue of explicitly stated rights.

On the other hand, there is a looming issue at the heart of the project: will the new Constitution, drafted and based upon concepts of principles of the eighteenth, nineteenth and twentieth centuries, and its future building blocks, be able to cope with the challenges of the coming decades? How does this Constitution fit with the emerging constitutional doctrines of European law, and indeed, global law?

The answer to these questions essentially depends on whether the fundamental structure of the new Constitution will be able to absorb such challenges and adapt to them inherently or explicitly by way of future amendment and change. Apparently, the underlying idea of the project is that, once adopted, different parts and pieces may be revised and replaced by amendments in due course, following the examples which the government in the field of direct democracy and the judiciary has already prepared. Challenges, however, may exist to the overall structure of the Constitution. In this case, its adoption in effect runs the risk of setting us back. Indeed, once adopted, it will be difficult to change its fundamentals in the coming decades. It would then be better to preserve the existing, albeit somewhat messy document. It will be seen that this problem primarily exists in relation to the federal structure of the Constitution.

Towards a five-storey house of constitutional law

I would like to approach this question once again from the angle of an international lawyer, primarily dealing with European law and international economic law. This is an unusual angle to look into national constitutional law. Yet, it is my belief that future framework conditions of national constitutions and political systems will be substantially influenced by these regulatory levels. National constitutional law, as we know it, has to cope and interface with more recent layers.

As a framework of analysis, I would like to conceive of constitutional law as a five-storey house. While we have been familiar with the first, second and third storeys, the constitutional levels of the communes, the cantons or sub-federal entities, and of the federal structure, fourth and fifth levels are currently being added.[14] The fourth amounts to the framework of regional integration, in particular the EU and its treaties. This level exists whether or not the country is a member of the Union, as it is obliged to adopt laws and regulations in conformity with European law in order to minimise trade barriers and transaction costs. A fifth and emerging level is global. I am thinking here of emerging structures of global integration in the field of trade regulation, in particular within the World Trade Organisation (WTO) and the Bretton Woods institutions. While this is still embryonic, it is likely that the rule of global law, effective dispute settlement and enforcement of rights, will gradually develop constitutional and supranational structures binding upon states and also organisations of regional integration. Other international fora, perhaps the United Nations, may emerge in response to global regulatory needs, and call for adjustment both on the regional, national and cantonal level.

In this five-storey house, it is evident that national constitutions are bound to remain centres of power in coming decades. This is true outside of the EU, but also within it, and of course, also with regard to global structures. Nevertheless, regional and global integration increasingly influence the role and function of national constitutions, quite in the same way as they, in the nineteenth century, fundamentally changed local and cantonal constitutions of formerly true sovereign entities. Needs and functions of the national constitution will change, and also affect the first and second storeys. Let me give two examples.

Firstly, regulating the scope of government intervention in economic activities has been at the heart of the constitutional debate in 1848 and 1874, and ever since.[15] The question arose both in terms of state intervention on the part of central government, and in terms of remaining regulatory competencies of the cantons in this field. The Constitution deals with these boundaries in a fair amount of detail, even if important conceptual questions have remained open. The point I wish to make is this: with regional integration and global economic integration, the thrust of these issues is now being addressed on the fourth and fifth floors of our building, i.e. the European and global levels. Requirements for interventionism by national and local governments are set forth in detail in the European Communities. Moreover, in the law of the WTO, these boundaries are set forth partly in even more detail. For example, the basic rules on subsidisation of agricultural products, of exports, of research and development today is essentially regulated on the fifth level[16] and need no longer take centre stage in the national Constitution. In fact, especially with regard to the allocation of regulatory powers between the federal government and the cantons, it may therefore be advantageous to leave these questions flexible in order to facilitate structural adjustments in the wake of regional integration and globalisation.

The draft Constitution, however, allows regulation of the economy only to the extent explicitly provided for in the Constitution, and limits economic policy regulations beyond policing and competitively neutral measures by cantons to monopolies (Art. 85: 3 DC). The cantonal powers are extremely limited, in other words, in providing measures of structural adjustment. For example, a canton would be barred from supporting ailing industries by its own structural adjustment programmes, even if WTO law allows it to do so. At the same time, existing constitutional guarantees to intercantonal market access – the equivalent of Art. 30 EEC – has been removed from explicit individual rights and is left to legislation (cf. Art. 23 and 86: 2 DC, and short of bringing about free movement of persons in public functions outside the private sector). Even though no fundamental change is envisaged, this might lead to a weakening of the constitutional aspect of individual market access.[17]

Given the fact that economic activities are increasingly regulated at the level of regional and global integration, regulations on the third floor should be reviewed and possibly made more flexible, leaving much more to the level of legislation and governmental programmes. It no longer makes sense to prescribe a straitjacket, by means of federal constitutional law, to determine what the cantons are, and are not, allowed to do, in terms of economic policies in their specific responses to structural adjustments in the wake of European and global integration processes.

My second example relates to a somewhat opposite constellation: instead of transferring regulatory powers to the fourth and fifth floors of the building, regional and global liberalisation and market integration lead to new constitutional problems on the first, second and third floors. They bring about new tasks which, in the past, have not existed to the same extent. I am talking here of integrating foreign, non-European individuals and families and their cultural background. With the globalisation of the economy and of communications and decreasing costs for transportation, traditional communities have to cope with an increasing number of foreigners. Switzerland has become a destination of immigration, not so much for Europeans, but from cultures overseas.[18] It is one of the drawbacks of regional integration and globalisation that nations and national constitutions are called upon to provide for enhanced social and economic integration of foreigners. Rights and obligations of this segment of the population – amounting to some 20 per cent in Switzerland – need to be addressed and better defined in constitutional law. The Constitution should not remain silent with respect to one-fifth of the population. True, most human rights standards are applicable to all humans, independent of their nationality and are thus unlike the field of political rights. Similarly, social standards and goals in the Constitution do not distinguish on the basis of nationality (yet legislation often does so). But is it enough in a constitution, setting forth the fundamentals of state activities and public responsibilities, merely to retain the principle of *non-refoulement* (no turning back) (Art. 21: 2 DC) and to state otherwise that legislation on foreign nationals is a matter for the federal government, and moreover, that foreigners may be extradited if they are a risk to national security (Art. 112 DC)? Would it not be essential to recognise the core functions of integrating foreign nationals and residents, to establish principles, rights and obligations, to provide for programmes and set forth the interaction of federal, cantonal and also communal responsibilities in this field? The Constitution has to be a factor of integration not only for nationals, but for all humans living under its umbrella in a given society. I am fully aware that these are extremely sensitive issues, but can we afford to remain silent on that point in the nation's founding document?

These two examples may demonstrate that the present reform by its very nature of merely updating the Constitution does not and cannot adequately deal with the challenges of the twenty-first century.

We have to be aware that this is a project essentially looking back and up to the present, but not into the future. At the same time, these are examples which could possibly be dealt with by traditional means of future piecemeal revision, even though provisions on economic regulation are spread through the document. It would seem possible to continue traditions of piecemeal, bottom up and pragmatic constitutional policies within the new framework.

The fundamental problem of allocating powers

The problem, however, does not end here. While a number of current and future issues can be addressed and adapted piecemeal, there are limits to this when it comes to the fundamental structure of the eighteenth-century traditions of the Federal Constitution. The traditional pattern of allocating powers between the cantons and the federal government and its perpetuation in the draft Constitution will inevitably cause difficult regulatory problems and tensions with the fourth and fifth levels of the constitutional building. The current reform process, although aiming in the right direction, therefore does not go far enough.

Following the traditional model of power allocation, powers of the federal government need explicit enumeration, while the cantons otherwise remain uninhibited or formally sovereign (Art. 4 DC). In economic regulation this was virtually reversed, and cantons are, as I have pointed out, extremely limited by the Constitution. The Constitution thus adopts a pattern of allocation which follows the ideal of assuming the responsibilities for separate tasks and walks of life. The tasks assigned to the federal government are all listed in the Constitution, while those of the cantons are sometimes, and unnecessarily, mentioned (for example, cultural heritage, Art. 62, culture, Art. 83, except for radio and television, Art. 76). In many of these areas, implementing powers and the power to enforce are attributed to the cantons. In terms of regulatory powers (jurisdiction to prescribe), however, we hardly find the model of mixed competencies in the draft Constitution. It essentially follows a model of exclusive and clear regulatory attributions in different domains and within particular domains, respectively. Exceptions and joint responsibilities can rarely be found, for example, in the field of internal security (Art. 53 DC), and in the administration of highways (Art. 67 DC).

This model of allocation of regulatory powers perfectly fits a three-storey house, contained in the nation state. However, it is bound to run into problems in a five-storey house with law-making on the regional and global levels increasing. This is so for the following reasons. More and more fields are addressed by rules of European and international law. Looking at regulatory approaches both in the EU and on the global level of the WTO and other international fora, it is important to note that these regulations are rarely of a comprehensive nature. They address key issues and points necessary to bring about the degree of harmonisation required with a view to overcoming, for example, excessive trade barriers. International regulation, therefore, is piecemeal and needs to be complemented, if not implemented, by rules of the first three floors of the constitutional building.[19] More importantly in the present context, international rules do not respect and follow allocations of powers in a given federal structure. Agreements, regulations and directives of the EU may partly affect jurisdiction of the federal government, and partly of the sub-federal entities, the cantons in Switzerland. As a matter of international or European law, the federal government is responsible for implementation and compliance. As a matter of federal law, it does not have explicit jurisdiction to compel cantons to implement and comply with rules falling under their jurisdiction. It is controversial whether such powers exist implicitly, and there are good arguments in favour of such powers.[20] Yet, as a matter of constitutional practices and traditions (which are of paramount importance in the absence of constitutional judicial review of national legislation), the federal government has constantly refrained from the exercise of such powers, and there is no doubt that such exercise would cause considerable political problems. As a practical matter, the third storey cannot successfully enact implementing legislation in these domains. The federal government may thus enter into agreements for the cantons where domestically it has no established jurisdiction to prescribe and enforce such rules.

The increase of international and supranational rules thus bears the potential of considerably shifting and upsetting the balance of traditional constitutional patterns. The distinction between federal and sub-federal tasks is being eroded. cantons are not satisfied with this erosion, and have reacted in seeking stronger impact on international treaty negotiations. Such powers are granted under Article 50 of the DC which codifies a current trend in constitutional practices.

The federal government and level, however, is equally frustrated since it does not have the powers to implement and enforce such obligations, yet has to assume international responsibility. A good and telling example in this context is government procurement.[21] In Switzerland, overall rights and obligations are defined by the WTO Agreement on Government Procurement. Since the federal government has only very limited powers to regulate the matter for the cantons, it only enacted a comprehensive bill on government procurement for the federal entities. Limited rules on non-discrimination are contained in the recent internal market bill, partly with differing rules (in social standards) from the Federal Procurement Act. The cantons undertook to harmonise the matter in an interstate compound, partly inconsistent with the internal market bill, and further legislation exists within the cantons of communities on the matter. The federal government has no powers to enforce compliance of international obligations within the cantons.

It is interesting to observe that similar and comparable problems also arise on the fourth constitutional level, the European Union. Obligations incurred under the WTO partly affect areas for which the EU domestically does not have any competencies. A good example is the Agreement on Trade Related Intellectual Property Rights[22] which also contains a substantial portion on civil and administrative procedures, for which the EU does not have any internal jurisdiction to regulate. These provisions enlarge responsibilities of the EU in external relations, but leave the matter to Member States domestically, and the EU has no jurisdiction to enforce these rules contained in a so-called mixed agreement while assuming responsibilities in external relations.[23] Again, the internal allocation of powers is being disrupted by rules of the fifth constitutional level. The model of enumerated powers ends up quite messy.[24]

It is submitted that classical allocations of mutually exclusive powers, following a division of different walks of life between a federal and cantonal level, or the European and national level, no longer can be maintained in the light of increasing international regulation in particular on the fourth and fifth floors of the constitutional building. Traditional structures come under stress. Vice versa, important international agreements may be opposed simply because they cut into traditional fields of cantonal competencies. It is apparent that the allocations of powers between the federal government and the cantons will further erode in coming years and decades in the wake of international harmonisation, both on the European level and on the global level. Tensions and frustration will occur. Cantons will be afraid of losing their regulatory powers, and the federal government will face the problem of how to implement and enforce international obligations. All of this is, of course, not a particular Swiss problem. It is apparent that emerging regulatory needs on the global and regional level deeply affect traditional allocations of powers. This is less of a problem in centralised states such as the UK or France, unless devolution becomes more extensive. But it is a problem in federal countries. The same problems arise in the Federal Republic of Germany and possibly Austria. Interestingly, Member States of the European Union face similar problems in defining allocations of powers among themselves. This lies at the heart of the debate of subsidiarity.

What we will find in coming decades are regulations relating to a particular walk of life which will be partly addressed on the global, partly on the regional, and then partly on the domestic level. Different walks of life will be addressed on different levels and storeys of the law at the same time, and the legal system has to be able to integrate these levels and make them operational as a whole. It will be a matter of finding the most appropriate constitutional level for regulating a particular issue. This suggests that classical and exclusive allocations of powers between different federal levels should be given up to the benefit of a model of mixed competencies in the field. It would therefore seem necessary to find new ways of allocating domestic regulatory powers and the criteria hereto.

Remedies

It is apparent that the draft Federal Constitution, as much as the existing one and the EU treaty based upon a concept of enumerated powers, cannot bring about a more flexible allocation and pre-emption of cantonal powers. This is a matter which affects the fundamental structure of the Constitution. It will not be open to subsequent piecemeal amendments. The concept of Article 3 DC cannot be changed without changing a substantial portion of the Constitution. The adoption of the present draft will be there to stay. While piecemeal reform will continue, it will be impossible to change its fundamental structure. Switzerland therefore runs the risk of adopting an outdated structure which will not be able to cope with the normative and regulatory approaches emerging for the twenty-first century. The same holds true for Community law where solutions compatible with global regulations need to be designed.

It would be more suitable to allow the federal government to enact framework regulations (*Rahmengesetze*) in *all* regulatory matters. It is too late, indeed, to make this fundamental point. The train cannot be stopped on this ground. What can and should be done? Do we have to reject the draft Constitution because of these fundamental deficiencies to cope decently with the demands of the fourth and fifth floors of the building?

One is first tempted to do so. Yet, the problem is not one of the draft. It is one of constitutional traditions. Quite clearly, proposing a flexible and more centralised allocation of powers, such as the inter-state commerce clause in the USA, would bring the project down in a referendum. You cannot make fundamental changes in time of peace and short of existential crisis. The previous draft, proposing flexible allocations in 1977, failed. All we can therefore attempt to do is to temper the effects of the traditional allocations of power and provide for tools which may render it more flexible in coming decades without rewriting the fundamental rules.

One approach to compensate for the loss of powers due to inter-nationalisation of law-making is to reinforce the role of the cantons and of the communities, in particular of large cities and agglomerations, in foreign policy-making. It can be argued that established federal states, such as Switzerland, will increasingly learn from somewhat more flexible constellations within the European Communities. Paul Taylor claims that the relationship is revealed by the notions of *symbiosis and consociation*, rather than strict separation of regulatory domains and tasks.[25] Indeed, the structure of the Communities has been characterised by strong involvement of Member States in decision-making which in return has allowed for more flexibility in job allocation. The more Member States have a (strong) say in Community legislation, the less important clear-cut allocations of powers are. In the light of the key role of the Council, it is therefore not astonishing that the doctrines of implied and inherent powers, as well as unanimous extensions of competencies in Art. 235 EC Treaty, are much broader than in Switzerland. It was only with the advent of majority ruling and the increasing impact of the European Parliament that the idea of subsidiarity arose and then became a household name. Job allocation therefore is inherently linked to *decisional processes within the respective constitutional level*, and it is here, in my view, that remedies should be sought in the first place.

It is interesting to observe that sub-federal entities, for reasons of compensating lost autonomies, increasingly reinforce their say at the federal level also in matters of foreign affairs and at the fourth floor of Community legislation.[26] Particular efforts to reinforce the role of the cantons in foreign policy in Article 50 DC have already been mentioned. Legislation to formalise the role of cantons is under way while the role of cities and larger agglomerations remains to be addressed. The drawback is that new informal constitutional layers in the decision-making process are being created, by the so-called Inter-cantonal Conference (KdK), and it remains to be seen whether complications can be successfully managed in the context of international relations.

A bolder step would consist of returning the Senate (Conseil des Etats) to the original role of this Chamber and link the mandate more closely to the cantonal governments and also provide a forum within or outside of this Chamber for better representation of cities and agglomerations in the political process. Given the emerging structure of law-making across different constitutional layers, the assurance of adequate representation of the first and second storeys at the third level should be re-established. The future lack of exclusive jurisdiction to prescribe can be procedurally compensated by appropriate representation at higher echelons of the constitutional order. Whatever the results will be, it is evident that the cantons will emerge with a somewhat stronger position on the third, federal constitutional level. It is interesting to observe that we can already see a certain convergence with structures of the European Communities in this respect.

A second instrument to deal with the problem of implementation simply is a policy of direct effect of international agreements. This means that private persons and actors may directly rely upon such agreements in defining their rights and obligations. While such self-executing effects are, of course, widely achieved in EU Member States in relation to the fourth floor, i.e. Community law and thus after Swiss membership is achieved in the future also relevant with regard to cantonal law, it has not yet been established and achieved with regard to global law.[27] The dualist system of the United Kingdom is an example in point. Adopting, where suitable, direct effect of international agreements, however, will allow the enforcement of international obligations by cantonal and federal courts even if the canton or commune fails to implement a particular obligation. This is an important point since direct effect is mostly opposed by federalist, i.e. decentralising forces, as they believe they can obtain more political leeway with such a strategy. However, they ignore that direct effect in fact could help to limit legislative intervention of the federal government, as courts of law would look to international agreements being respected and implemented, rather than the federal legislator. This is an angle which defenders of cantonal autonomy should take to their hearts. It would be advisable to enshrine the principle of *primauté* of international law and reinforce the doctrine of direct effect under the traditions of Swiss monism. Such a principle does not exclude exceptions in specific areas, in particular where fundamental rights are adversely affected by international or European law.[28] Whether or not these complex relations are explicitly introduced into the Constitution is perhaps of less importance as long as the Supreme Court continues to support the doctrine of direct effect – perhaps with a new federal angle set out above.

To the extent, however, that direct effect is excluded or impossible, and implementation is required, it would seem suitable to bring about a more flexible allocation of powers, allowing the federal government to prepare and co-ordinate implementing legislation for international agreements and obligations. It is therefore advisable that a more flexible allocation of powers be introduced in the Constitution to the effect that the matter is being regulated by European or international law. This could become a horizontal provision affecting all federal and cantonal and communal tasks. It could find its place in the context of article 3 DC, or in fact Article 3 of the existing Constitution: 'To the extent that matters of a cantonal competence are being regulated by international agreements or in European law, the federal government assumes the powers to enact, if necessary, implementing legislation and to assure compliance with international law to the extent that international rules are not being considered self-executing.' To the extent that this goes too far, such powers could be limited to cases where cantons have failed to implement obligations incurred on their own initiative after the lapse of a certain period of time.

Conclusions

The long-standing effort at reforming the Federal Constitution seems to confirm the impression that the process has not been a very exciting experience. Firstly, it is apparent that fundamental constitutional changes during peacetime and the absence of unrest are not possible. An overhaul of the Constitution is limited to what is called *mise à jour* or *Nachführung* which does not entail the ambition to bring about shifts in the allocation of powers and competencies. Secondly, the Swiss experience also demonstrated that constitutional reform is still undertaken in a self-contained framework of national constitutional law. The implications of regionalisation and globalisation were not sufficiently present throughout the discussions.

The shift to European and international law because of the increasing need for regional and global rules, forces a rethinking of the proper role of national constitutions. Based on the experiences with Swiss constitutional life and reform, I suggest that the concept of constitutional law be broadened beyond the nation state and that the matter be considered in terms of a five-storey house. From local, to cantonal, federal, regional and global levels, it is a matter of allocation of powers and jobs to the most appropriate level. By doing so, it is no longer a matter of allocating entire regulatory domains, but of pertinent aspects of each of the domains. A domain may be partly regulated by different levels at the same time. We need to rethink the models and patterns of traditional allocations of powers between central government and the sub-federal levels. New models of allocations are needed which allow each level to have its regulatory share in the subject matter concerned and are flexible enough to absorb the evolutions on the regional and international level. We therefore need to think hard where detailed and where open-ended rules best serve the community at large. The core functions of the national constitutions in the twenty-first century will be to mediate between the different levels and allow for *symbiosis and consociation*.

Based on this model, it would seem at first that basic changes are imperative. Adopting a constitution that does not consider these facts puts us at risk of not being fully prepared for the challenges of the new century. To some extent, remedies and adjustment to new challenges may be introduced henceforth on a continued piecemeal basis. To some extent, however, responses are more difficult to find and could only be addressed through fundamental changes in the structure of constitutions. An ideal federal constitution would look considerably different.

At the same time, it is not of great help to suggest completely new designs which the political process in times of relative stability and peace cannot absorb. We need to work with existing traditions and seek to introduce tools allowing the interface with international and European law to operate smoothly. Hence, there is no reason to reject the new draft Constitution. Yet, the interpretation of the present Constitution either in its old or new dress and further work with, and thinking about, the Constitution should be accompanied by new underlying approaches to constitutional law. Perhaps this is the most important lesson we can learn from the Swiss experience.

In constitutional practices, interpretation and future reform, the evolution of regional and global law requires more flexible allocations of power between the federal and cantonal levels, as much as between national, regional and international law. With the traditions of enumerated powers, more flexibility in constitutional practice can be achieved by reinforcing representation of cantons and municipalities on federal levels. Switzerland may learn from European Community structures which, despite relying upon enumerated powers, are more flexible due to a strong participation of the Member States. First, enhanced participation of the cantons and the agglomeration on the levels of federal decision-making, including a reshaping of the Conseil des Etats, is a promising path which should be pursued. Second, it is important to establish a nuanced doctrine of constitutional hierarchy of norms stemming from different layers of the constitutional order. The doctrine of direct effect, including direct effect of global law, will be of assistance in supporting traditional allocations of power between the different layers. Third, an adequate doctrine of implementing rules of different layers needs to be developed.

It will be interesting to see how constitutional law in Switzerland will evolve, after the adoption of the new Constitution in 1999, which came into effect on 1 January 2000. More important than the document creating a constitution for the twenty-first century, however, will be the change in attitudes towards constitutions and their

interpretation in the light of the new five-storey house. In all countries and federal states, it requires broader and different perceptions
and attitudes, fully integrating the new fourth and fifth levels which
represent new dimensions of constitutional law.

Acknowledgements

I am indebted to Professor Clive Church for comments on a previous
draft, and Daniel Wueger (Berne) for critical comments and assistance in preparing the present text.
The essay was completed before the results of the parliamentary
debates in December 1998 were known and the final draft Constitution was made available by government.

Notes

1. In a recent presentation, Valéry Giscard d'Estaing put it like this:

   Vous êtes, en effet, comme nous, les citoyens de notre grand continent.
   Vous êtes entourés de tous les côtés par l'Union Européenne et vous con-
   stituez en réalité, vous en Suisse, un laboratoire avancé de nos problèmes.
   Vous pratiquez, en effet, avec bonheur, le multilinguisme; vous connaissez
   une très forte décentralisation; vous mettez en pratique depuis longtemps,
   le principe 'théologique' de la subsidiarité; vous assurez sur votre vie pub-
   lique un contrôle démocratique efficace; vous faites fonctionner, enfin, une
   confédération dotée d'institutions centrales, d'une monnaie, d'une politique étrangère et d'une politique de défense indépendantes. On pourrait
   croire qu'il suffirait de regarder la Suisse avec une loupe fortement grossis-
   sante pour réussir à organiser l'Europe.

   See Valéry Giscard d'Estaing, *L'Union Européenne. Elargissement ou appro-
   fondissement?* (Basler Schriften zur europäischen Integration No. 34, Basle,
   1997), p. 6.
2. Clive Church, letter of 2 November 1998 to the author.
3. In 1997, of the total amount of imports and exports Switzerland imported
   78.8 per cent from, and exported 61 per cent to, the EU. See Report on Swiss
   Foreign Economic Affairs 1997, *BB1* (Federal Reporter) 1998, I, p. 878 and
   Thomas Cottier, 'Das Ende der bilateralen Aera: Rechtliche Auswirkungen der
   WTO auf die Integrationspolitik der Schweiz', in: Thomas Cottier and Alwin
   R. Kopse (eds), *Der Beitritt der Schweiz zur Europäischen Union: Brennpunkte*

und Auswirkungen; L'adhésion de la Suisse à l'Union Européenne: Enjeux et Conséquences (Zurich, 1998), pp. 107, 108.

4. See Jan Atteslander and Ernst Baltensperger, 'Auswirkungen eines Beitritts zur Europäischen Union auf die schweizerische Finanzpolitik', in: Cottier and Kopse, *Der Beitritt der Schweiz* (see note 3), p. 696.

5. See *The Economist*, 3 October 1998, p. 38.

6. For an excellent account see Wolf Linder, *Swiss Democracy: Possible Solutions to Conflict in Multicultural Societies* (London, 1994).

7. Wolf Linder, 'Erfordert die Mitgliedschaft in der Europäischen Union eine Anpassung des schweizerischen Regierungssystems?', in: Cottier and Kopse, *Der Beitritt der Schweiz*, p. 428.

8. See Jörg Paul Müller, *Die Grundrechte der Schweizerischen Bundesverfassung*, 2nd edn. (Berne, 1991). A third edition is in preparation.

9. See *Bericht der Expertenkommission für die Vorbereitung einer Totalrevision der Bundesverfassung* (EDMZ [Govt. Printing Dept.] Berne, 1977), pp. 110–19.

10. By now, five cantons have completely revised their constitutions (Solothurn, Thurgau, Glarus, Berne and Appenzell-Ausserrhoden), while ten others have started projects to do so (Ticino, Grisons, Lucerne, St Gallen, Fribourg, Zurich, Neuchâtel, Schaffhausen, Vaud and Basle-Stadt). See *Botschaft über eine neue Bundesverfassung, BB1*, 1997, I, pp. 53–64.

11. See Andreas Kley, *Der Grundrechtskatalog in der nachgeführten Bundesverfassung*, presentation to the Bernese Law Association, in: *Zeitschrift des bernischen Juristenvereins*, vol. 135 (1999) (forthcoming).

12. In its initial proposals, the government suggested a substantial increase of the number of signatures needed for a referendum (from 50 000 to 100 000) and for an initiative (from 100 000 to 150 000). In addition, two new mechanisms were proposed: a general initiative which would give parliament the power to decide whether it prefers to enact a statute or propose a constitutional norm, and a new type of financial and administrative referendum which allows for specific (non-law-making) decisions of parliament to be put to the vote. In addition, it has been proposed to extend the referendum with relation to treaties. See Federal Council, *Reform der Bundesverfassung: Verfassungsentwurf 1996* (EDMZ, Berne, 1996), pp. 82–9; *Erläuterungen zum Verfassungsentwurf* (EDMZ, Berne, 1995), pp. 205–44). Another proposal, submitted by the Social Democratic Party, aims at introducing the so-called constructive referendum. This would allow changes of the proposed statute to be advanced instead of simply vetoing the entire bill. These proposals are under discussion in parliament. It is unlikely that the changes will materialise within the concept of the *mise à jour*. They may be taken up at a later stage upon adoption of the new framework.

13. In particular, there is a project to reform governmental structures and the administration. It has sometimes been called *Project D*, and is likely to progress with a view to seeking membership of the European Union. Further information about this venture can be found at the webpage: http://www.admin.ch/ch/d/rvr/index.htm.

14. While I originally thought about a four-storey house, I was convinced at the conference that the communes, having substantial powers of their own, should be added – even if this has not been a traditional way of looking at the matter. The expansion of constitutional notions beyond the traditional levels of the canton and the federal government towards regional and global structures, also suggests a refinement of domestic levels and gives a complete picture of the entire building.

15. The introduction of an individual and constitutional right to economic freedom (*Handels- und Gewerbefreiheit, Wirtschaftsfreiheit*) in the first revision of the Swiss Constitution in 1874 was a reaction to protectionism still exercised by the guilds after the adoption of a liberal constitution in 1848. See Müller, *Grundrechte* (note 8), p. 352; for a historical account see also Thomas Cottier and Benoit Merkt, 'La fonction fédérative de la liberté du commerce et de l'industrie et la loi sur le marché intérieur suisse', in: P. M. Zenruffinen and A. Auer (eds), *De la Constitution. Mélanges J. F. Aubert*, Basle, 1996), p. 449.

16. See, for example, the WTO Agreement on Agriculture which, together with tariff schedules, defines the scope of domestic support, market access and export subsidisation to a much more detailed degree than federal constitutional law. Another example is the Agreement on Subsidies and Countervailing Measures which, in the field of industrial goods, entails detailed rules on admissible scope of governmental support measures. See *The Results of the Uruguay Round of Multilateral Trade Negotiations, the Legal Texts* (Geneva [GATT Secretariat], 1995), pp. 438 and 264, respectively, and *passim*, as, indeed, the case could be made for virtually all the WTO Agreements, including services and intellectual property regulation. For an assessment of WTO law in Switzerland see Thomas Cottier and Krista N. Schefer, 'Switzerland, the Challenge of Direct Democracy', in: John H. Jackson and Alan O. Sykes (eds), *Implementing the Uruguay Round* (Oxford, 1997), pp. 333–64; and the same authors' 'The Relationship between World Trade Organization Law, National and Regional Law', *Journal of International Economic Law*, vol. 1 (1998), pp. 83, 108–10.

17. See *Botschaft über eine neue Bundesfassung* (note 10), pp. 289–302.

18. See Thomas Straubhaar, 'Auswirkungen des freien Personenverkehrs auf die Migration in Westeuropa', and Didier Chambovey, 'L'impact potentiel de la libre circulation des personnes avec les pays de l'Espace économique européen sur les flux migratoires en Suisse, both in: *Swiss Papers on European Integration*, vol. 4 (Berne and Zurich, 1996), pp. 13 and 37.

19. On this point and related matters, see Thomas Cottier, 'Die Globalisierung des Rechts – Herausforderungen für die Praxis, Ausbildung und Forschung', *Zeitschrift des bernischen Juristenvereins*, vol. 133 (1997), p. 217.

20. See Valentin Zellweger, *Völkerrecht und Bundesstaat* (Berlin, 1991), pp. 88–90.

21. See Thomas Cottier and Benoît Merkt, 'Die Auswirkungen des Welthandelsrechts der WTO und des Bundesgesetzes über den Binnenmarkt auf das Submissionsrecht der Schweiz', in: Roland von Büren and

Thomas Cottier (eds), *Die neue schweizerische Wettbewerbsordnung im internationalen Umfeld* (Berne, 1996), pp. 35–86 (with an Annex containing the WTO Agreement on Government Procurement in English, p. 163).

22. *The Results of the Uruguay Round of Multilateral Trade Negotiations* (note 16), p. 365.
23. See Opinion I/94 of 15 November 1994, [1994] ECR I-5267.
24. In *Hermès International*, the first case dealing with the interpretation of the TRIPs Agreement as a mixed agreement and thus of shared powers between the EC and the Member States, the Court was asked to construe Dutch civil procedure rules in the light of the TRIPs Agreement. The Court affirmed its jurisdiction on grounds that, while the Community has no jurisdiction in civil procedural matters in general, similar questions arise in the context of the proper EC trade mark regulation, *Hermès International v. FHT Marketing Choice BV*, 16 June 1998, Case C-53/96, [1998] ECR (not yet reported). The case is typical for the dilemma arising from the idea of separate competencies in the light of the fifth global constitutional level. It makes perfect sense for the Court to address the interpretation of the TRIPs Agreement with a view to achieving an overall coherent application of its norms. At the same time, the reasoning adopted by referring to Community trade mark law in order to bring about jurisdiction is hardly convincing. It should be found on grounds that the Court has jurisdiction to construe all international agreements concluded by the Communities, whatever their subject matter.
25. Paul Taylor, *The European Union in the 1990s* (Oxford, 1996), p. 181.
26. See generally Rainer J. Schweizer and Stephan C. Brunner, *Die Mitwirkung der Bundesländer an EU Vorhaben in der Bundesrepublik Deutschland und in Österreich: ein Modell für die Mitwirkung der Kantone in der Aussenpolitik*, 14 Swiss Papers on European Intergration (Berne and Zurich, 1998).
27. On this topic see Cottier and Schefa, 'Switzerland' (note 16).
28. For this approach see the jurisprudence of the German Bundesverfassungsgericht in the so-called 'Solange' cases, BverfG 37, pp. 271ff., 73, pp. 339ff. and the Maastricht judgement of the Court, BverfG 89, pp. 155ff. Similarly, the Swiss Federal Council stated in its report on the accession to the Agreement on the European Economic Area in 1992 that the *primauté* of EEA law would be restricted to the extent that it is at odds with basic principles of law or with the core of human rights ('Grundprinzipien und Kerngehalte der Grundrechte'), *Botschaft zur Genehmigung des Abkommens über den Europäischen Wirtschaftsraum, BB1*, 1992, IV, p. 92.

5
Swiss Politics Today

Wolf Linder

In the past, Switzerland was famous for the excellent quality of its watches, cheese and other industrial goods, or for its unique but rather expensive tourist sites. Its economy provided continuous growth; even in the first crisis of the 1970s official unemployment rates rarely reached more than 2 per cent. Besides, Switzerland was known for its somewhat particular democracy. On one hand there is no change of the role of government and opposition, on the other people vote on important decisions from speed limits for cars to the abolition of the army. Third, and probably most important of all, Switzerland has always been a reference model for political stability. For almost 40 years now, the Swiss government has been composed of the same oversized coalition of four political parties, which hold together about 75 per cent of the seats in parliament.

On the international scene, Switzerland followed a strategy of political neutrality. This meant that the Swiss were economically integrated in the Western economy but did not participate either in NATO or the EU or even in the UN. In the times of the Cold War, this political neutrality was welcome to the big powers: Switzerland was armed but no threat to anybody. Because of this non-involvement in world politics, the Swiss were seen as dependable trustees and negotiators: Swiss diplomacy discreetly maintained contacts between Americans and Cubans after the USA had closed its embassy in Fidel Castro's Havana, or brought together political antagonists from the First, Second and Third World in a Geneva hotel suite.

In the past 10 years, things have profoundly changed. In the polycentric world which emerged after the end of East–West antagonism,

Swiss neutrality is not needed any more. In 1992, the Swiss became the victims of their historical conviction that 'keeping out by going alone' is always best for a small country: the people voted against participating in the Single Market Treaty with the EU, and four years later, they decided against participating in peace-keeping operations of NATO. Even though the Swiss government has tried to tie Switzerland closer to the EU through bilateral agreements on the most important questions of trade, the negotiations were tough. They resulted in the agreements reached at the end of 1998 in the seven following areas: overland transport, civil aviation, free movement of persons, research, public procurement, technical barriers to trade and agricultural products. Despite these agreements, many say that Switzerland has manoeuvred itself into a position of self-isolation. This not only with regard to its relation to the EU but also with its armed neutrality which is regarded with renewed suspicion: if Switzerland does not participate in the European system of collective security, it is considered a free-loading parasite.[1]

In the last two years, Switzerland has come to realise that this isolation is no longer as splendid as it used to be. Swiss banks as well as the Swiss government have been heavily criticised for their collaborative policy on gold trade with the Nazi regime and for withholding restitution to Nazi victims after the Second World War. The activities of New York Senator D'Amato and some Jewish organisations culminated in efforts to boycott Swiss banks in the USA. 'Bashing Switzerland' has become fashionable. The Swiss image of 'good governance' has changed.

Even Switzerland is nowadays experiencing the effects of globalisation. World-wide liberalisation of trade, driven through by the World Trade Organisation, makes protection of agriculture more difficult.[2] Many policies – transport, energy, public services – have had to be adapted with deep changes made to their structures. The Swiss economy has lost many of its former advantages. At the same time unemployment has risen, farmers and lorry-drivers are upset, rich Switzerland has announced the phenomenon of 'new poverty' and growing inequality; like people in every other industrialised country the Swiss too have to work more to gain less.[3] All this taken together shows a dramatic societal and economic change. In every other country, I suppose, this would lead to a change of government, to big electoral swings in the party system, or to the emergence of new parties. But this is not the case in Switzerland. Despite the crucial changes, the grand coalition of the four political parties – the Radicals, the Christian Democrats, the Social Democrats and the People's Party, remains uncontested in national elections.

I would like to interpret this phenomenon from a political scientist's point of view and discuss the following questions:

- How can a government survive such serious crises without losing power? Why is there no strong opposition to take over with the promise 'to do better'?
- Is the political stability of Switzerland with its power-sharing system of four parties not the sign of an unresponsive political system? Can such a system still be defined as a democracy if regular change of power between political parties does not seem possible?
- Is direct democracy an obstacle for a nation state which needs to adapt to the deep changes induced by the process of globalisation or internationalisation?

In order to discuss these questions, let me first give a brief description of direct democracy and power-sharing in Switzerland.

The Swiss have the unique privilege not only of electing their parliament every four years but of participating directly in certain political decisions. This is possible through two devices. The first is the referendum. It allows the people to challenge any parliamentary decision: in a *votation* open to all citizens, the people have the last word whether or not a parliamentary bill will be accepted. The second device of direct democracy is the so-called popular initiative. A group of 100 000 Swiss citizens can, by their signature, submit to the government a proposition for constitutional change. After discussion of the request in parliament, the people vote. For instance, in September 1998, the Swiss voted on two popular initiatives and on one referendum:

- they refused a popular initiative to maintain the old privilege of women receiving their pension three years earlier than men, that is, at the age of 62 instead of 65;
- they rejected a special system of subsidies for small farmers;
- they accepted a new lorry tax, which has the ecological effect of moving long-distance transport of goods off the road on to the railways. The Swiss people vote on about ten national issues every

year. To this, you have to add referenda and popular initiatives at the cantonal and local level. One could say that Switzerland lives in the middle of a permanent voting campaign. Table 5.1 details the actual use of referenda and popular initiatives.

The effects of direct democracy, however, should not be exaggerated. Basically, Switzerland is a parliamentary democracy like most countries are. Yet, the system of representation has been extended to direct participation of the people in the most important parliamentary decisions. You can compare this with driving a car: parliament and executive keep the motor running and choose the direction. The people sometimes intervene: when using the referendum and saying no, they stop the car by applying the brakes. Parliament then has to try again to override the obstacle. Or the people press the accelerator by handing in a popular initiative.

The direct effect of the referendum is immediately felt: the braking device causes a considerable slow-down in policy-making, on the political left as on the right. On the one hand, in the 1970s, when we

Table 5.1   Referenda and popular initiatives at the federal level, 1848–1997

Obligatory referenda	
Went to a vote	188
Accepted by the cantons and the people	140
Refused	48
Popular initiatives	
Proposals handed in	217
Withdrawn or lapsed	74
Pending in 1997	22
Initiatives proceeded to a vote	121
Initiatives accepted	12
Initiatives refused	109
Counterproposals proceeded to a vote	13
Counterproposals accepted	6
Counterproposals refused	7
Optional referenda	
Bills subject to referendum	1889
Challenges by referendum	129
Parliamentary bill successful	62
Challenge by referendum successful	67

observed a Socialist swing in Europe, the development of public spending or social programmes was comparatively modest in Switzerland. On the other hand, in the early 1990s, when neo-liberalism was at its peak, the referendum prevented welfare programmes from being cut to a minimum. The accelerator effect of the popular initiative is less effective. Only 10 per cent of the initiatives are accepted by the people. Thus, this device is of little use in planning revolutions, but sometimes it has effects even when voted down by the people. For example, the popular initiative to abolish the army in 1989 received only 36 per cent of 'yes' votes. The government however, understood that it was spending too much on the army and since the vote the military budget has been cut considerably. Nonetheless, the impact on daily politics is not the only effect of direct democracy. Probably even more important is the fact that the referendum has induced profound changes in the political system as a whole. It made majoritarian modes of politics impossible and led to the consensus democracy of a permanently oversized coalition.

The reason is simple. Every pressure group or political party feeling discriminated against by a parliamentary decision can challenge that new law. The risk for the political majority of losing a referendum is high, especially if many groups are dissatisfied with a new bill. In order to avoid such risks, the government, before presenting its bill to the parliament, invites all potential referendum groups to participate in the preparation of a new law. For the same reasons, the government is composed of an oversized coalition. This allows the integration of the bigger political parties and gives the parliament a better chance to reach a sufficient majority which can avoid or win a referendum. Thus, political decisions in the Swiss system are always a compromise between different groups, a compromise also between different cleavages that characterise Swiss society: Left versus Right, urban versus rural areas, Catholics versus Protestants, or German-speaking majority versus French-speaking minority.

We call this system *Konkordanzdemokratie*, a term which indicates the proportional representation and the participation of all important political parties in the government. It also means the integration of all the relevant groups and the permanent striving for political compromise in parliamentary decision-making. The referendum even compels the political parties to co-operate. This was exactly the experience of some cities or cantons, when the political right or the left and Green parties tried to abandon all-inclusive coalition politics in order to form a simple majority government of the Right or the Left. The fierce use of the referendum by the opposition made it impossible for them to realise their electoral programme.

That concludes the first part of the answer why, despite dramatic changes in Switzerland, there has been no change of government in the last 40 years. The reason is: direct democracy. Direct democracy forces an oversized governing coalition to co-operate in order to minimise the risk of challenge by referendum. Certainly, one could take the view that Swiss democracy is a cartel, unresponsive to the will of the voters because they have no influence on the composition of the government. And without the periodic interchange of government and opposition as in the UK, there is no real democracy. There is some truth in this assertion. I shall try to give two answers to this. First, consider the voter. The Swiss system offers two opportunities to exercise political influence. One by elections, the other by participation in popular initiatives or referenda. From what I have said so far, it is absolutely clear that elections in Switzerland provide no big influence because the government is not likely to change, even with considerable electoral volatility. But with direct democracy, the influence of the voter is maximised in the concrete situation of important singular political decisions. The voter can decide whether or not to agree with the government's proposition to join the EU, to have a new tax system, or at what age one receives his or her pension. Voters' influence by election is minimal, influence by *votation* is maximal, and I would say that this is exactly the opposite of what citizens are used to in the UK. My hypothesis is that one cannot have it both ways in the same system. There is a trade-off between influence through election and *votation*, which is shown in Figure 5.1.

My conclusion is that even though we both speak of democracy, the UK and Switzerland are different worlds of democracy (see Table 5.2): after elections in the UK, the country can undergo a considerable political change, and even the stock market reacts when Tony Blair defeats John Major. The British system maximises the influence of the voter through the electoral process. Swiss elections, on the other hand, are not even worth a mention in the *New York Times*. But the result of a popular initiative to abolish the Swiss army makes headlines.

Citizens' influence

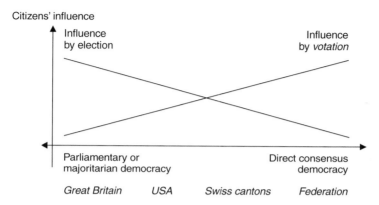

Figure 5.1 Citizens' influence by election and votation in parliamentary and direct consensus democracies.

Table 5.2 A comparison of representative and direct democracies[6]

Great Britain: Representative system	*Switzerland: Semi-direct democracy system*
Competition between parties and their governments. Winner takes all	Co-operation of all political forces in government. Proportional representation
Periodical alternation of power because of elections	Negotiation and power-sharing in legislation. No alternation of power
Political legitimation through changes in power or re-election of government satisfying voters' expectations	Institutional legitimation comes from participation: the most important decisions being taken by the people, important ones by parliament and the rest by government
Enactment of the political programme of the majority	Integration of pluralistic values, minorities and of group interests; different coalitions on major issues
Policies for the people	Politics through the people
Participation as a form of general and programmatic influence: voters elect a government and its programme for the entire legislative period	Participation as a form of 'one-issue' influence: people vote on specific questions. No strategic government policy

Second, consider the Swiss cartel regime. Comparative political science has shown that the Swiss system of *Konkordanz* is not unique at all. The Dutch/American political scientist Arend Lijphart has found that co-operative government in oversized coalitions exists in quite a few countries. He calls this 'consociationalism', or 'power-sharing', or 'consensus democracy'. It is another type of democracy, differing in many respects from 'majoritarian democracy' for which the Westminster model is the archetype. Lijphart[7] has tried to identify the essential, distinguishing elements of majoritarian and consensus types of democracy, and has found the following:

The majoritarian (Westminster) model:
1. Concentration of executive power: one-party and bare-majority cabinets
2. Separation of powers, formal and informal
3. Balanced bicameralism and minority

4. Two-party system
5. One-dimensional party system

6. Plurality system of elections

7. Unitary and centralised government

8. Unwritten constitution and parliamentary sovereignty
9. Representative democracy

The Consensus Model:
1. Executive power-sharing: grand coalitions

2. Fusion of power and cabinet dominance
3. Unicameralism or asymmetric bicameralism representation
4. Multi-party system
5. Multidimensional party system
6. Proportional representation
7. Territorial and non-territorial federalism and decentralisation
8. Written constitution and minority veto

When trying to fit 21 countries into this model, he found a wide spectrum of democracies characterised either by elements of majoritarian or consensus democracy (Table 5.3). Thus, majoritarian and consensus democracy can both be considered as democracies, working differently and giving particular institutions a different function. Both have their specific advantages and disadvantages.

Table 5.3 Majoritarian and consensus democracy: nine clusters of democratic regimes

| | | Dimension II (Federalist structure) | | |
		Majoritarian	*Intermediate*	*Consensual*
	Majoritarian	New Zealand United Kingdom	Ireland	Australia *Austria** *Canada* Germany *United States*
Dimension I (Political Process)	*Intermediate*	Iceland *Luxembourg*	*France V* Norway Sweden	*Italy* Japan
	Consensual	Denmark *Israel*	*Belgium* *Finland* *France IV* *Netherlands*	*Switzerland*

* Plural and semi-plural societies are italicised.

Table 5.4 Political integration and innovation[9]

	Consociational direct democracy	*Competitive parliamentary system*
Political integration	High	Low
Political innovation	Low, slow continuous	High, fast discontinuous

One of the most discussed questions is the relative performance of the two types of democracy. For a long time, the common wisdom was that consensus democracy is strong with respect to integration, but weak in innovation. With majoritarian democracy, it is the reverse: it is characterised by strong innovation and weak integration. This can be represented as shown in Table 5.4.

The latest comparative studies indicate that the hypothesis of weak innovation in consensus systems is not necessarily true. As Hans Keman from Amsterdam or my colleague Klaus Armingeon in Berne can show, consensus democracies in Europe have not had a weaker performance in economic and social policies in the last 20 years.[10]

This could be due to the fact that consensus democracy avoids the stop–go politics which characterise some majoritarian systems. Our understanding of the effects of majoritarian and consensus democracy is still limited. What we can say, however, is that analogies with the market system are misleading: those liberal theories that state that a political system, like the market system, works best with tough competition cannot be verified on empirical grounds.

There exists another argument in favour of consensus democracy. Politics is more than economic performance. It is also a matter of dealing with different cultures. As Samuel Huntington points out, the world-wide political conflict of the next decades will be the clash of civilisations.[11] And some say we are already in the midst of this conflict, as all countries are subject to a growing global migration and are therefore becoming more and more multicultural. This brings me back to Switzerland. Switzerland was a multicultural society from the beginning. It is culturally heterogeneous, historically split into four languages and two religions. To overcome these cleavages, power-sharing with minorities was essential. It has helped the Swiss to develop a national identity, to survive in times of external threat, and to participate in the economic growth in the favourable conditions of the European economy after the Second World War. Finally it permitted the integration of our own native minorities. And this is probably the most important argument: for culturally split societies, consensus democracy has some essential advantages. Minorities, who will never have a voice in a majoritarian system, can be integrated in a consensus system by power-sharing, that is by participation and co-operation. No wonder that elements of consensus democracy can be found not only in old segmented societies like the Netherlands, Belgium or Switzerland, but also as a key to the solution of multicultural conflicts in South Africa or in Northern Ireland.

Consensus democracy, however, has its price. While it permitted the integration of our own minorities, it did not help very much to integrate foreign workers in Switzerland who constitute 20 per cent of the population. Consensus democracy needs lengthy negotiations, and often, the compromise is far from a clear-cut decision. Swiss politics, in the last decade, have not always proved capable of grasping the opportunities offered by the accelerating changes of globalisation. Globalisation, not membership of the EU, is the real challenge for Switzerland. Unlike the EU question, Swiss citizens cannot vote whether they want to take part in the process of globalisation. Switzerland is already part of it, and it also means that questions of national interest, hitherto the subject of popular participation, are decided elsewhere, in Brussels, New York, in Vienna or London. This is not good news for the ordinary citizen; unlike politicians and members of parliament who win new seats and mandates in international organisations or in the EU parliament, the citizens lose their voice. Thus, the refusal of the Swiss people to join the European Economic Area must not only be interpreted in terms of economic advantages and disadvantages. Citizens feel that with the process of European integration and globalisation, they are losing part of their influence in politics.

This takes me to my last question: what about the future of direct democracy? Will the referendum and the popular initiative continue to play an important role in Swiss politics, or is it a device that is becoming obsolete in the process of globalisation? I have already given one part of my answer: globalisation diminishes the autonomy of the nation state, leads to the growing interdependence of foreign and domestic policies, and shifts politics away to transnational organisations and authorities like the UN, EU, OSCE (Organisation for Security and Co-operation in Europe), WTO or others. This loss of national autonomy reduces the influence of national parliaments in general, and in Switzerland it also diminishes the effects of direct democracy. Nevertheless, this is not a one-way street and represents only one part of the answer. Direct democracy leads to decisions of strong democratic legitimacy, and this strong legitimacy can be used by the Swiss government in its relations with Europe. This can be illustrated with the case of transport policy, an important issue in the bilateral negotiations between the EU and Switzerland.

For some 20 years now, Switzerland's strategy in transport policy has been influenced by ecological considerations. This meant investing in public transport instead of roads, and it meant higher taxes for petrol, cars and lorries, thus favouring public transport instead of individual motoring. This policy led to some difficulties with the EU. EU transport policy officially is as much ecological as the Swiss, but in practice it was much more dictated by the road-haulage lobby in the Netherlands, Italy, Germany or Spain. It demanded free access and free road transport through the Swiss Alps, which provide one of the three important throughways on the north–south axis of continental

Western Europe. The Swiss are willing to construct two new tunnels through the Alps, thus expanding capacity to handle the growing north–south transport in the Single Market. But these two tunnels are to be constructed for railway transport, and the Swiss rejected proposals to establish enlarged capacity on the road. Moreover, in 1994 the Swiss accepted a popular initiative that demanded higher tolls for lorries crossing the Alps, in order to get them on to the railway. It came to open conflicts between the EU and Switzerland. The overland transport question was the most difficult of all the seven issues in the bilateral agreement between the EU and Switzerland, and the last to be resolved after four years of negotiations. The Swiss delegation was considered to be stubborn, but the Swiss representatives tried to explain that the option for a public transport solution was the people's will that could not be questioned in diplomatic negotiations. Some observers say that this strong position has even begun to influence the transport policy of the EU itself. This illustrates the fact that direct democracy can have considerable impact in the transnational arena.

From a more theoretical point of view, one should not underestimate the risks of such a policy. As long as direct democracy was primarily concerned with domestic politics, it was a dialogue between a people and its government. The people could say no the first time, the government would propose its second or third project and finally the people would say yes. In international relations, direct democracy becomes more complicated. Here there are three actors to consider: the Swiss government, its people, and the international authority or supranational organisation. If the people reject the result of the government's negotiation, this can be a risk. The reason is evident. The international agency or organisation will not need the Swiss as much as the Swiss government needs its people. Therefore, the international agency will not lose too much time in negotiating a second or third time. The negotiating power of the Swiss delegation could then be diminished, or the international actor will have no interest at all in continuing further negotiations.

As every other country, Switzerland today has to cope with the crucial changes induced by internationalisation and globalisation. Its polity, and its structures of decision-making are not optimal for managing rapid change. Its decisions take a long time, radical changes in national policy occur rarely. When refusing to participate in the

European single market, the Swiss missed the chance of political integration in Europe, and despite the risk of isolation or of economic disadvantage, it will take a long time for the Swiss to abandon their traditional view of 'going it alone'. Not for the first time in their history, the Swiss are refusing to follow the crowd.

The system of direct democracy and power-sharing in Switzerland provides decision-making structures that persist. This might be a handicap in a time when quick decisions in national as well as in international politics are necessary. On the other hand, these structures have their own qualities. They have an integrating effect which is important if our multicultural society is to keep its identity and unity. And so far, the slow pace of power-sharing has not provided bad results in terms of social and economic policies.

One last point. While the decision-making structures of direct democracy and power-sharing could have some disadvantages for Switzerland in the next decade, they are receiving increasing attention in other countries. Consensus democracy is attractive for new democracies in Eastern Europe and in Africa. However consensus democracy is not like a recipe on how to cook a cheese fondue. Every country has to experiment in its own way with the basic presuppositions of its own culture. As to direct democracy, it seems to have become fashionable. In Germany as well as in Eastern and Central Europe, more and more referenda on the local or national level are taking place. It might be that 30 years from now, direct democracy will not remain the defining characteristic of the Swiss, but will be considered as a possible way to develop new methods of democracy everywhere.

Notes

1. See Günter Bächler (ed.), *Beitreten oder Trittbrettfahren? Neutralität in Europa* (Chur/Zurich, 1994), and Alois Riklin, 'Isolierte Schweiz: Eine europa- und innenpolitische Lagebeurteilung', *Schweizerische Zeitschrift für politische Wissenschaft*, 1 (1995), pp. 11–34.
2. See Thomas Cottier, 'Zwischen Integration und Weltwirtschaft: rechtliche Spielräume der Schweiz nach der Uruguay-Runde des GATT', in Wolf Linder *et al.* (eds), *Schweizer Eigenart – eigenartige Schweiz. Der Kleinstaat im Kräftefeld der europäischen Integration* (Berne, 1996), pp. 231–44.

3. See Wolf Linder, *Schweizerische Demokratie. Institutionen, Prozesse, Perspektiven* (Berne, 1999).
4. Ibid., pp. 244ff.
5. Ibid., p. 133.
6. Ibid., p. 132.
7. Arend Lijphart, *Democracies. Patterns of Majoritarian and Consensus Government in Twenty-one Countries* (New Haven, 1984).
8. Ibid., p. 219.
9. Linder, *Schweizerische Demokratie*, p. 136.
10. Hans Keman, 'Politische Konsens und Konzertierung: Innenpolitik und die Festlegung politischer Grundsätze in Westeuropa', in *Schweizer Eigenart – eigenartige Schweiz*, pp. 85–107; and Klaus Armingeon, 'Konkordanz, Sozialpartnerschaft und wohlfahrtsstaatliche Politik in der Schweiz im internationalen Vergleich', ibid., pp. 69–84.
11. Samuel P. Huntington, *The Clash of Civilisations* (New York, 1996).

6
Finding a New Role in International Conflict Resolution: Switzerland after the End of the Cold War

Andrew Williams

An Englishman writing about a country with such a long and separate history as Switzerland must always begin by showing his bona fides. Switzerland is a country that I have come to like and admire over the years, as much for its failings as for its obvious successes. My interest in the topic under discussion in this essay is personal as well as academic. During the period that I lived in Switzerland in the 1970s and 1980s I spent a modest proportion of my time engaged in what we would now call 'second track' (i.e. unofficial) third-party conflict resolution activities, mostly within the framework of the Second Cold War of the early 1980s.

The main theme of this essay derives from my interest in seeing how Switzerland has managed to combine its internal political debates with its projection as a state. It has managed to create what I would call a 'mediatory society' and it has tried to used this internal experience to make a significant contribution to the resolution of the many conflicts around it and in its dealings with other states and non-state entities and groups. Geography has allied itself with experience to teach Switzerland how to survive so long in an essentially hostile world by being useful to others while enriching itself. The most obvious example of that lies in another area of Swiss excellence, finance and banking, where Switzerland now has 'two of the world's top banks, the second biggest reinsurance company and the third biggest life insurance company'.[1] Yet Switzerland is now facing a crisis in its foreign policy, to the point where a Swiss diplomat told me in the early 1990s: 'We now have no foreign policy.' Even allowing for a certain hyperbole, we must ask what he meant, whether it is still true, and, most of all, from what heights of success did he think they had fallen?

Switzerland has managed to survive so long because it has always taken on board what my former boss, Jacques Freymond, liked to refer to as 'le living–learning process'. The country's rulers have been forced to combine the resolution of their internal conflicts with a constant interest in other peoples' problems. They have had to do so because Switzerland is so small and so surrounded. If it had not it would have been swallowed up by the linguistic giants to its north, south and west many years ago. As a consequence of this need Switzerland has punched well above its weight in the field of international conflict resolution since at least 1945 and particularly since 1975. I would therefore argue that it is in Switzerland's vital intrinsic domestic national interest to be good at conflict resolution and to develop new abilities in this area as the external environment changes.

Before setting about trying to demonstrate the evidence for these assertions it is necessary to make one or two methodological points. As many of my readers will know, the very nature of conflict resolution makes it difficult to analyse. Those who have conducted such activities cannot just talk about what has been done and who it has been done with. Extramarital affairs are conducted with far less secrecy than conflict resolution activities – unless they happen to be in the White House of course. To add to this dilemma of description and analysis, Switzerland is a particularly secretive society – as the practices of the Swiss banks illustrate. It is not easy to have an inside track on what is being planned in Berne or on the ground in Swiss missions abroad. I have perhaps had a particular insight due to my connections with Jacques Freymond (often referred to in my day as 'le conseiller fédéral non-élu') but I cannot fool myself that I am an insider. These are the comments of a nosey foreigner, albeit one who is a frustrated *Vaudois*.

A first task has to be to say what is meant by the assertion that Switzerland is a 'mediatory society'. To do this requires at least some consideration of what Switzerland has meant over the last 50 years or so. The central fixed point in these 50 years, indeed of at least the last 150, has been Swiss neutrality. This neutrality, is, along with the concomitant militia army and the greatest food shop on earth, La Migros, both the greatest strength and the greatest weakness that Switzerland brings to its attempts to influence the rest of the world.

The downside of this neutrality is most commonly stressed in the public mind of the rest of the West, and derives from a widespread perception that Switzerland's neutrality has insulated it from the 'real world'. Many in the West, and indeed in the rest of the world, have tended in recent years to criticise Switzerland for its wealth, its self-satisfaction and its supposed secrecy and isolation. It is considered by many to have hidden behind the skirts of the Allies in two world wars and to have profited from others' misfortunes in those wars. To a certain extent all stereotypes have their justification – I shall never forget being told by an old Swiss lady in 1975 how terrible it was when in 1943 (*sauf erreur*) an American bomber accidentally dropped its load of bombs on Carouge, a suburb of Geneva. My childhood was marked by family stories of whole areas of Britain being devastated by bombs. My mother even had a German fighter pilot land on her house – naturally she made him tea until the Home Guard turned up. My father had his house demolished by a bomb while he sat 50 feet away in a shelter made of corrugated iron and dirt.

On a wider level, it is easy to poke fun at the efforts of a small neutral state trying to make sense of a global war in which it might so easily be swallowed up. But the truth is more stark. As the most definitive account of current Swiss thinking on military and foreign policy (the Brunner Report of February 1998) has it: 'From 1815 until 1945 Switzerland was permanently in the centre of continental lines of tension. Latent conflicts between its neighbours led to three wars within a hundred years.'[2] There was a real danger in both world wars that Switzerland would be overrun by the armies of Germany or France, or indeed possibly of the United States or Soviet Russia, as happened in the Napoleonic period. All of these states put enormous pressure on Switzerland to join their camp and all of them used it as a neutral ground for the most extravagant of unofficial discussions with their enemies. For example, Allen Dulles, the founder of the OSS (later the CIA) conducted extensive negotiations with the denizens of Heinrich Himmler in Berne to try and bring the war to an early close. Russian and other spy networks sprouted on Swiss soil in ways that John Le Carré would be hard put to describe.

So why was neutrality seen as so essential for the survival of the Swiss polity? The main reason lies in the real dangers of a centrifugal disintegration in times of crisis. Swiss society had the obvious potential of becoming hopelessly divided in its loyalties, especially given the linguistic, cultural and religious barriers that have existed and continue to exist between the Francophone, Germanophone and Italian-speaking areas. The citizen of *la Suisse Romande* still refers to the area 'outre-Sarine' in tones of hushed horror. When I first saw this river Sarine I was most disappointed not to have to go through a Swiss Checkpoint Charlie. However, the barriers are psychological if all the more real for that. As another great Swiss, Denis de Rougemont, once said to a very young Andrew Williams, 'if you think that myth is less real than "facts" you are sadly mistaken'. If I did not fully understand him at the time, I do now. As the conflict in the former Yugoslavia has shown, the mix of cultural difference that is Switzerland and many other states can so easily explode into ethnic violence. The pictures that we see of Kosovan or Bosnian villages in flames could very easily be scenes from the Valais or the Graubünden. The chalets are identical in all but their fixtures and fittings.

Switzerland has dealt with such tensions by developing a system of democracy at home and neutrality abroad that seems to other European states both quaint and cumbersome. It is only with reference to this system that we can understand how Swiss neutrality has been a force for good not only in Switzerland itself but also beyond. To explain this I need a short detour into Swiss politics.

The real level of power within Switzerland is not at the level of the state but of the commune and the canton. This can be illustrated by other methods than the usual dictum that 'most Swiss have no idea who their President is'. Until quite recently federal income tax was referred to as an 'impôt pour la défense nationale', and it was a mere fraction of the total tax take. So on the level of the most important effect that a state can have in peacetime, the citizen perceives his local government as more important than his central government. If a commune wants to delay a federal initiative, it can do so and often does. The commune of Bex in the Valais held up the entire motorway-building programme in the Rhône valley for years because it did not like the proposals on offer, so we all had to drive to Bex where the motorway stopped in the middle of field full of cows and go back on to the old road for a few miles. As you will all know, referenda (*votations*) are common for everything from abolishing military service to rebuilding a hotel frontage. The Swiss get so fed up with this that they often do not bother to vote. But as result of this, no conflict can fester, everyone has their say, and the result is a creative chaos that suits a people who are both conservative and fiercely independent.

Historically, this has preserved the peace when the rest of Europe was in flames. William Lloyd, in a study of Swiss mediation which went back to 1291, concluded that 'conciliation and mediation were a fundamental part of political relations between the cantons almost from the beginning and any analysis of the causes for the Swiss success in sticking together more or less peacefully and finally achieving full federation must take these practices fully into account'. Lloyd considered that only these practices prevented the centrifugal forces of religious intolerance doing what they did to the rest of Europe. He also made the important point, relatively novel when he was writing in 1963, that powerful states and organisations like the United Nations often cannot play a mediatory role, and that 'launching peacemaking initiatives should be the valid concern of the unaligned nations'.[3]

The problem is that running a foreign policy with a democratic citizenry is very frustrating. They do not like being led, only widely consulted. For example, the Swiss Foreign Ministry has (on the whole) been a fervent supporter of entry into the European Union for many years now, and it has also favoured entry into the United Nations. It has been constantly frustrated in these ambitions. I for one am not in the least surprised, and part of me agrees with the bloody-minded logic that makes the mountain fastlands of *la Suisse profonde* so deeply suspicious of extraterritorial bureaucracies that neither care for nor share the traditions of democratic extremism that has kept Switzerland safe for many generations. Switzerland might have almost invented the expression 'self-reliance'. Its population well understand the African proverb: 'When the elephants fight, the grass suffers; when the elephants make love, the grass suffers just as much.' Perhaps it is better to keep well away from elephants?

Neutrality therefore has its benefits, but the price has also been very high. Given the frustration felt by many in Berne over many years with the seeming incomprehension by its population of Switzerland's deep interdependence with the rest of Europe, the Swiss government has been forced to be inventive in its attempts to influence those whom its citizenry seem to reject. One crucial way that it has done this is to act behind the scenes in virtually every conflict since 1900, not as a principal participant but as a third party that can smooth the path to peace. To show how this happens I shall talk first of the tools of such activity and then of the evidence for it happening.

What are the tools of Swiss third-party activity? The most obvious and well known outside Switzerland is the International Committee of the Red Cross. While in theory and practice a non-governmental organisation, one of the reasons for the great respect in which it is held, the ICRC is nonetheless a quintessentially Swiss organization. It is quietly efficient, very low-key and has played a key role in every major conflict this century. By so doing it has bought immeasurable solace to hundreds of thousands of prisoners of war and prisoners of conscience. It has also played an unostentatious role in countless minor dramas, whether they be in the taking of hostages, negotiating refugees through roadblocks, or saving prisoners from torture or execution. It continues to do this on a daily basis. Countless human lives have been saved by ICRC personnel. It should not be forgotten that virtually all of their volunteers in the field are young Swiss men and women, the only exception to that being the use of some non-Swiss medical personnel. To join the ranks of these brave young people is the highest and often the normal aspiration of many young Swiss. I have many friends who have served in such a capacity, and I know of some who have given their lives for this ideal.

Another key tool has been through the many international (or more correctly intergovermental) organisations that exist today. The League of Nations was set up on Swiss soil and the UN still has its European headquarters there. The physical location of the UN in neutral Geneva has made the city the scene of some of the most important third-party activity since the 1920s. It was in Geneva, for example, that much of the preliminary work for what became the Lancaster House Agreement on Zimbabwe took place. I can perhaps date my own interest in other people's conflicts to the day in 1979 when I was nearly bowled over by an irate Ian Smith, then Rhodesian Prime Minister, who had stormed out of talks with Robert Mugabe in the UN building with the cry 'Bad light stopped play!' I was then surrounded by about 40 Japanese journalists to whom he had shouted this strange phrase demanding that I explain the rules of cricket – and I was only on the way to the library!

I shall allude briefly to other kinds of Swiss activity within international organisations below, but it is clear that the reason why Switzerland asks for such extremely low rents from the UN and the specialised agencies is so that it can continue to influence world events in the *ambiance feutrée* of the UN. Its main competitor to host such agencies has been another small, neutral and mountainous country, Austria. The logic is the same: the ability to exert influence while ostensibly staying out of other people's quarrels.

A third way that Switzerland has played a vital role in resolving conflicts has been in the use on a number of occasions of important Swiss personalities by the major powers to resolve their seemingly most intractable problems. For example, the Swiss played an important part in the Evian Agreement of 1962 that ended the Algerian War of Independence. During the Cold War this became an institutional involvement that has been called an 'active neutrality'. This play on words, it should be noted, was never meant to evoke an absolute 'neutral' stance – Switzerland has been a full member of the 'West' since 1946, and its war games always included a 'red' army and a 'white' one. There are few prizes for what this ultimately meant. The French word *engagement* is here perhaps most useful, for from the Second World War Swiss foreign policy can be characterised as a *neutralité engagée*.

Much could be said of the history of Swiss third-party activity up to the Second World War and during it, but I have written about that elsewhere and there is not the space to go into it here.[4] It is nonetheless worthwhile thinking a little about what Switzerland achieved in the area of conflict resolution during the Cold War itself. Again Swiss self-interest and global interest have been served in a particular way.

Clive Church and I were invited in September 1996 to a conference celebrating the 50th anniversary of Churchill's famous Zurich speech of 1946, in which he first spoke publicly of a 'United States of Europe' and the need for a Franco-German *rapprochement*. While the world remembers this speech for those wise words, the Swiss remember it as bringing them out of their isolation, an isolation that had started in 1939. Once the Cold War got under way, after another Churchillian prediction at Fulton, Missouri, in the same year of 1946, Switzerland started to play a role that gave it and the other neutral powers an enormous amount of quiet leverage.

There were various ways in which this happened. Jacques Freymond describes how the first opening came in the early 1950s with an invitation to Switzerland to take part in the armistice arrangements in the Korean War, and especially in the repatriation of prisoners of war – a traditional Swiss occupation. During those discussions Switzerland progressively saw itself put forward, along with the Swedes, as a 'Western neutral' (*neutres de l'Occident*), while the Soviet Union promoted Czechoslovakia and Poland in the role of Eastern neutrals. During later crises of the Cold War – Suez and Hungary in 1956, and the Algerian War – the Swiss played a particularly important part as mediators.[5]

In all of these matters Switzerland benefited from an easing of tensions as refugee flows diminished and the threat of terrorist action on Swiss soil was reduced. The country has never forgotten the assassination of Empress Elizabeth of Austria, the Princess Diana of her day, in front of the Hotel Beau Rivage in the 1890s or the Cheka activities of the 1920s that saw blood flow in the streets of Lausanne. Such things still happen, as we saw when Iranian assassins gunned down the leader of the exiled *mujahedin* on the Route du Lac not far from Geneva not so long ago. If the Swiss do not export their skills of conflict resolution, the conflict has a tendency to affect them at home. This is enlightened self-interest writ large, but no less beneficial for all that.

But it was with the period of détente that Switzerland saw its real chance to influence events. It is often remarked that the process that we might say culminated in the 1975 Helsinki Final Act and the establishment of the Conference on Security and Co-operation in Europe was mainly of benefit to the United States and the Soviet Union. The former was given official sanction to interfere in the internal affairs of the Soviet Union in the area of human rights, the latter thought it had achieved a peace treaty to confirm its hegemony over Eastern Europe. I would rather point first to the role of the Swiss in setting up the CSCE and its subsequent function as intermediary between the elephants of the African proverb I cited. Thus the Swiss have done their bit to keep Europe peaceful and the grass has largely stayed intact and grown very lush indeed. The Swiss achieved this success by helping to create a group of like-minded states, from East and West, known as the 'Neutral and Non-aligned' group within the Helsinki process.

It was during this period that I had my first personal experience of conflict resolution, Swiss style. Swiss academics, including Jacques

Freymond, had played a certain facilitating role in Helsinki in the years leading up to the signature of the Final Act, as had Soviet and other nationals based in Geneva. As the Second Cold War deepened in the aftermath of the Soviet invasion of Afghanistan and the Polish emergency, the Madrid Conference of the CSCE (1981–83) saw its proceedings increasingly disrupted by mutual distrust and acrimony. It was actually suspended for over a year, although that was at least partly due to the actions of Malta. I had the task of going to the Madrid Conference and trying to get the delegates to consider the idea of a Cultural Forum. An unlikely task for a young Englishman, one might think. Well, I was astonished to find that a Swiss 'mafia' had got me temporary membership of, of all things, the Vatican delegation and that I was presently visited by about half a dozen of the Geneva Graduate Institute's doctorate-holders, who all were now highly placed in the delegations of a number of key neutral, Western and East-bloc countries. (I cannot say which I am afraid, for obvious reasons.) After much discussion, I found myself chatting to a nice Russian who turned out to be a KGB general (a fact I discovered in 1997) and plotting the Cultural Forum, after which even the British Foreign Office deigned to notice my presence, but only to ask what the Russian had said to me. ('Secrets of the confessional, my son' was all I replied.) To cut a long story short, the Cultural Forum duly happened in 1985, at least partly due to these efforts.

What this taught me was that Switzerland works in mysterious ways its wonders to perform. It acts as an extended family and into this family during the Cold War were invited all those states in Europe who felt in any way threatened by that Cold War. Switzerland came to encapsulate the idea of 'active neutrality', especially during the tenure as head of the Swiss Foreign Office of Ambassador Eduard Brunner, a man of enormous intellect and influence. The Swiss made the CSCE almost their own organisation in some ways, and played a vital role in the subsequent evolution of the CSCE from an academic curiosity in 1975 to that of the central debating chamber for the end of the Cold War in the late 1980s.[6]

In a sense this meant that the end of the Cold War left Switzerland without a foreign policy, a perception which, as I mentioned earlier, was widespread in Berne in the early 1990s. The New World Order of George Bush was supposed to presage a new era of peace and harmony. The Neutral and Non-aligned group, within which Switzerland had played such a vital role, fell to pieces as Sweden, Austria and Finland rushed to join the European Union and effectively shelved their neutrality, while all the Eastern Neutral and Non-aligned countries clamoured to join either NATO and/or the EU. The balance of power in the revitalised CSCE (since 1994 the OSCE) moved to an East–West Axis and left Switzerland with nowhere to hang her hat. The Swiss people's refusal to join the UN, the EU or even the European Economic Area, led to the aforementioned mood of near despair in most of the federal bureaucracy. Worse still, the splits in the electorate were along seemingly linguistic lines with no prisoners being taken on either side of the Sarine. When to this was added a persistent economic recession, it is not without justification that René Lanzin said that 'the unsuccessful diamond jubilee [has been] combined with the not exactly euphoric 700-year anniversary'.[7]

However, all is not lost. The 'Oslo Channel' in the Middle East, where Norway has performed a vital role in the discussions between the Palestinians and Israel, has proved that small states can still make a real difference. The Oslo Channel benefited from the mediatory expertise of Norwegian academics and diplomats and provided the necessary framework for an actively neutral forum.[8] Why cannot Switzerland provide a similar framework in other circumstances, as it managed to do so successfully during the East–West conflict? After all, the threats that are the inevitable offshoots of conflict far beyond Switzerland's borders are as real as ever, in particular those of global terrorism, of insecure sources of oil and the risk of refugee flows. As the Brunner Report points out:

> These phenomena will probably increase in the decades to come. [...] They can undermine our confidence in the values of democracy and tolerance. They can weaken our conviction that the relations of power – at the national as well as at the international level – must be transparent and controlled and that conflicts, which cannot be avoided altogether, must be resolved peacefully. Our security begins with our demonstration to preserve these values and convictions and to see them respected all over the world.[9]

They have indeed attempted to do so. In Chechnya, during 1995–96, Swiss Ambassador Tim Guldimann conducted within the framework of the OSCE what Victor-Yves Ghébali calls 'une politique dynamique et courageuse' as an intermediary between the pro-Russian Chechens and those intent on independence. In doing so, he ran the risk of annoying the former who saw him as giving recognition to the enemy, and the latter who saw the OSCE as hostile to their aspirations.[10] He therefore undertook an extremely dangerous task, where there was a high risk of kidnap or assassination by one side or the other. It might be noted that President Yeltsin's personal adviser on the Chechen conflict was found dead while this essay was being written. It will be recalled that it was Yeltsin's representative of the time (1996), General Alexander Lebed, who brokered the ceasefire in Chechnya, but Guldimann and the OSCE under the Swiss presidency played an important preliminary role.

Might we now argue that the role of small states as go-betweens in European politics is over and that Switzerland must therefore find itself a new foreign policy? Perhaps the success of the West in the Cold War now means that the Swiss are victims of that collective success, one that they did much to broker in the Neutral and Non-aligned group of the CSCE in the 1980s? Much will depend on what Switzerland's role in Europe will be. Will it now be able to act better as a third party within a greater Europe, for example allowing the OSCE and the EU to avail themselves of its undoubted experience in conflict resolution and the provision of *bons offices*? It will obviously continue to be the home of the ICRC and the international organisations, which themselves play a vital role in all sorts of conflicts.

However, it must be said that the Swiss electorate's reluctance to have more than an arm's length relationship with the UN and the EU can only in the long run damage Swiss attempts at foreign policy projection. There is still only a very slim majority in favour of Swiss participation in UN peacekeeping activity being reported by opinion polls. Whenever this question has been put to the vote, those in favour have been outnumbered so far. In the case of the EU, a decade of sluggish economic growth has not persuaded the Swiss population to even sign up for the European Economic Area, a big step but one short of economic union with Europe. If that isolationist trend continues, maybe Europe will turn its back on the Swiss, especially if the international economy continues to deteriorate. In such times, free riders may find themselves without a horse.

Yet to join in with these clubs also poses obvious risks for Switzerland. Would not joining the EU and the UN mean losing its particular strength as a neutral – in short, becoming ordinary? Or is neutrality no longer an option in an interdependent world? Surely the Swiss banks have shown the way by voting with their feet and establishing much of their real activity in Luxembourg, London or New York. If the Swiss family is breaking up – and only time will tell – does this mean that the 'mediatory society' can no longer underpin a mediatory foreign policy or ultimately a successful polity for the next 150 years? That is the fundamental question facing the Swiss today, and it is one that will tax every ounce of their energy and ingenuity.

Acknowledgement

I should like to dedicate this essay to Professor Jacques Freymond who died in 1998. He was a great Swiss and an even greater European, whose benign and inspirational influence had a huge effect upon me and many others.

Notes

1. *Financial Times*, Special Supplement on Swiss Banking and Finance, 13 October 1998, p. 1.
2. 'The Geo-strategic Setting', *The Brunner Report* (Berne, 1998).
3. William B. Lloyd Jr, 'Mediation in Swiss History', *Council for Correspondence Newsletter*, No. 25 (April 1963), pp. 17–19.
4. Andrew Williams, 'The Role of Third Parties in the Negotiation of International Agreements', in: Chris Mitchell and Keith Webb (eds), *New Approaches to International Mediation* (New York, Westport, Conn., 1989), pp. 168–79.
5. Jacques Freymond, 'La Suisse face aux conflits', in: Max Petitpierre (ed.), *Seize ans de neutralité active* (Neuchâtel, 1980), pp. 143–53.
6. See Andrew Williams, 'Mediation by Small States: Some Lessons from the CSCE', *Paradigms*, 6/1 (Spring 1992), pp. 52–64.
7. René Lanzin, Editorial, *Swiss Review: the Magazine for the Swiss Abroad*, 6/1997, p. 3.
8. The most accessible account of this initiative can be found in Jane Corbin, *Gaza First: the Secret Norway Channel to Peace Between Israel and the PLO* (London, 1994).
9. See 'The Geo-Strategic Setting', *The Brunner Report*.
10. Victor-Yves Ghébali, *L'OSCE dans l'Europe post-communiste, 1990–1996: Vers une identité paneuropéenne de seécurité* (Brussels, 1996), p. 612.

7

The Swiss Economy: Facing the Future

Dominik Furgler

On the occasion of the 150th anniversary of modern Switzerland this year, we have spent a lot of time reflecting on the past. We have been studying the history of our country and its unique characteristics, recalling the achievements of our forefathers, asking ourselves how Switzerland has become what we know and experience today, and celebrating, holding speeches, organising seminars and workshops, and much more. That is all very well, as long as it does not serve to promote uncritical self-congratulation, the glorification of bygone days and the rejection of all that is new. It makes more sense to reflect as objectively and critically as possible (and by that I do not mean setting out from first principles to criticise) with the aim of gaining a better understanding of developments and thus modern-day circumstances, of inspiring us, and if necessary drawing lessons for the future; that is, a reflection which focuses on the present and the future.

On hearing the word 'Switzerland', the foreigner will naturally think firstly of cows, cheese, chocolate, watches, clocks – not to mention cuckoo clocks – and hopefully beautiful scenery and skiing too. These clichés are closely followed by banks, prosperity and the notion 'expensive'. Even if these concepts often involve stereotyped ideas and sometimes negative perceptions, they nevertheless all form a small part of a diverse, complex reality. And it is noticeable that they all reflect economic realities: industry, tourism, trade, financial services and economic strength. Although the individual does not consciously think in this way every time, he or she certainly associates Switzerland predominantly with economic factors. And even though Switzerland is much more, and has more to offer than its economy, this association is not incorrect. For in those 150 years of existence as a modern state, the Swiss national economy has evolved into a highly successful, competitive economy which is highly visible thanks to its strong international ties. And if people compare and contrast themselves with those of another country, then it is usually with regard to their prosperity. However the famous Swiss affluence – and thus the material foundation for the implementation by the state of social policies – rests principally on the success of our national economy.

I would like to indicate where this economy and its enterprises stand at the very threshold of the twenty-first century, and what the main challenges are for the economy and economic policy. I will start with a short review of the beginnings of our modern federal state from the economic point of view, then give an account of the current economic situation. Finally, I shall conclude with a few comments on Switzerland's competitiveness, that is, our strengths and weaknesses, thus identifying the challenges for the future.

Switzerland – like any country poor in raw materials – had to strive from the earliest times to provide circumstances which boosted the competitiveness of its enterprises and economy, and was reliant on capable politicians and entrepreneurs in order to do so. And in this respect it was particularly fortunate just around the time of the founding of modern Switzerland 150 years ago. Unlike many neighbouring regions, Switzerland was in some respects still a developing country with widespread poverty, child labour and appalling, recurrent famines; last century many people emigrated, never dreaming of the prosperity of today. The switch from an authoritarian confederation of states to a federal state based on direct democracy – a step which was revolutionary at the time in 1848 – was also based on substantial economic considerations. Fortunately, even then the links between economy and politics were close. For some of the leading industrialists in the land were among the leading politicians in the victorious liberal camp, and for economic reasons pressed for the creation of a federal state with a single currency, abolition of internal duties, the introduction of a unified system of weights and measures, and economic freedoms, creation of a state-owned post and so on. Thus the ambitious Swiss industrial sector of those times created not only ideal conditions for an undreamt-of economic boom at home as well as in foreign trade, but it also contributed to the establishment of political institutions and structures whose operation and stability had the effect of promoting the economy as well. I make this short detour back to the beginnings for three reasons: firstly, to recall that a strong economy and prosperity are not simply God-given, not even in wealthy Switzerland; secondly to stress the significance of courageous, responsible, forward-looking decisions in politics and the economy, and finally with an eye to the new challenges which confront Switzerland in the age of globalisation and the European Single Market, to which I will return later.

As I have already mentioned, Switzerland has no raw materials which could form the basis of industrial development. From the very outset, growth and prosperity could only be created by adding value – based on good ideas, specialisation, high levels of know-how and quality – in conjunction with cross-border trade, for the domestic market is too small. It is reasonable to assert, therefore, that factors such as professional qualifications and training, a modern infrastructure especially in the field of transport and communications, the use of modern technologies, the optimising of self-imposed conditions and defending liberal trade conditions and open markets have always played a very important role. Indeed, the latter has become the crux of Swiss foreign trade policy, for hardly any industrialised country can be as dependent on trade as Switzerland. It is therefore not surprising that Switzerland is particularly strongly affected by outside influences. Key concepts: globalisation, economic development and conditions prevailing in the most important trade partners, i.e. Germany and the EU. I will come back to this point several times.

It is necessary to begin with a brief look at the situation of the Swiss economy. Following six years of stagnation up to 1996, GDP increased slightly in Switzerland in 1997 with a modest rate of 0.8 per cent. The reasons for this were a high degree of dependency on other countries, the strong franc, economic problems in our partner countries, but also our own structural weaknesses and major problems in our domestic economy. The recovery of 1997 was above all due to external demand: the persistent strength of the world economy and the positive evolution of demand conditions in continental Europe, paralleled by the correction of the overvaluation of the Swiss franc, allowed for a strong acceleration in export growth in 1997. A positive development to be noted is that investments in equipment remain at a high level. Private consumption increased slightly during 1997 and even more in 1998. Registered unemployment dropped significantly to 3.5 per cent in August 1998. Statistical factors explain part of this decline. But, in recent months, broader measures of job seekers seem to indicate the first modest improvement in the overall employment situation. Despite rising import prices in 1997, consumer price inflation fell to an average rate of 0.5 per cent in 1997 and even 0 per cent in the first quarter of 1998. The recovery of the Swiss economy is expected to strengthen further in 1998. Exports will remain a major engine of the upswing, notwithstanding some slowing of export market growth caused by the Asian crisis and the strengthening of the Swiss franc in recent months. Solid export growth is increasingly supporting business investment and private consumption. Average GDP growth will therefore accelerate to a rate of 1.5–2 per cent in 1998.

Swiss exports of goods expanded by 7.7 per cent in real terms and by 11.6 per cent in value in 1997 to reach 105 billion Swiss francs. For the first time since a lengthy period of loss of market share on the world markets, the Swiss export industry was able once again to follow the rhythm of world trade growth. By destination, export growth was well balanced. But the strengthening of demand from EU countries gave the decisive impulse for export growth. In 9 of the 15 EU countries double-digit rates were reached. As a result, 60.7 per cent of exported goods were sent to the EU in 1997. In the EU itself, Germany accounted for 23 per cent of total exports, followed by France and Italy. With 5.8 per cent, the UK followed in fourth place. Overseas industrialised countries amounted to 15.4 per cent of total exports. The United States, with 9.8 per cent of total exports, are now clearly our second most important customer after Germany. With 3.8 per cent of total exports, Japan is far behind. Exports towards emerging markets of South-east Asia and Latin America amounted to 10 per cent of total exports (7.9 and 2.1 per cent respectively), whereas exports to countries in transition accounted for a somewhat lower share of 4.6 per cent (of which 2.1 per cent went to Central and Eastern Europe, the rest being shared between the CIS and other economies in transition like China with a rate of approximately 0.9 per cent each).

Export growth was also well balanced as regards sectoral distribution. At first, expansion was mainly supported by a surge in semi-finished products and consumer goods (chemicals, paper, plastics, clothes and jewellery). Yet, thanks to the recovery in the EU, exports of equipment finally took off as well. The sectoral distribution of goods exported shows that machinery represents 29.4 per cent, immediately followed by chemicals and pharmaceuticals at 28.2 per cent. These two leaders are followed by the metal and metalworks industry (8.6 per cent) and by the watch industry (7.9 per cent). Some sectors are heavily dependent on foreign markets such as the chemical and the machinery industries, whose exports accounted for more than two-thirds of total orders in 1997. Swiss companies are world leaders in several industries: food (Nestlé), pharmaceuticals (Novartis, Roche, Ares-Serono), speciality chemicals (Ciba, Clariant), electrical engineering and textile machinery (ABB, Saurer, Rieter, Sulzer), cement (Holderbank), watches (SMH), elevators/escalators (Schindler), temporary employment (Adecco) and testing and inspection (SGS). Interestingly enough, Swiss-owned textile machinery companies produced nearly a third of world output of this equipment in 1997. Yet only 40 per cent of the total came from factories in Switzerland. I shall return to the fact of foreign direct investment later.

In 1997, Swiss goods imported grew by 6.4 per cent in real terms and 12.1 per cent in value to reach 103 billion Swiss francs. This is explained by high dynamism in sectors not heavily dependent on the business cycle (for example, chemicals, pharmaceuticals and jewellery). But it is certainly also due to the improvement in domestic demand during the year, which increased the need for semi-finished products. Imports of telecommunications and information technology equipment have been especially high. By destination, 78.8 per cent of goods imported came from the EU in 1997; 32 per cent came from Germany, again followed by France, Italy and the UK (6.5 per cent). The sectoral distribution of goods imported shows that machinery represents 22.4 per cent of total imports, followed by chemicals and pharmaceuticals (16.3 per cent), vehicles (11.0 per cent), metal and metal works (8.7 per cent), agricultural products (8.6 per cent) and textiles (8.2 per cent). During the first four months of 1998, real imports grew, as compared to the corresponding period in 1997, by 6.9 per cent.

As more than half of the exports are produced in the two industries of machinery and equipment and of chemicals and pharmaceuticals, and as more than one-third of imports come from the same two industries, we may suppose that an important share of Swiss trade is intra-industrial. This fact demonstrates that the Swiss economy is fully participating in the globalisation of international business, consisting in an increased international specialisation of countries in different types of a given commodity from the same industry. For example, net services increased in 1997 as banking commission incomes took off. In addition, a fairly positive performance was registered in the tourism industry in 1997 with a growth rate of 4.4 per cent. This positive trend is explained by the weakening of the Swiss franc, the increased consumption in the most important countries of origin of tourists, and good weather conditions in autumn 1997. Net capital income clearly rose, thanks to rising direct investment and interest receipts. Therefore, in spite of the modest deterioration in the trade balance, the current account surplus once again rose in 1997 and exceeded the level of 1996 by 4 billion Swiss francs to reach more than 30 billion Swiss francs, which amounts to 8.3 per cent of GDP.

One cannot stress strongly enough that the EU represents the main foreign market as well as the main foreign supply market of the Swiss economy. Behind the global data, it is a fact that the EU constitutes, for many small and medium-sized enterprises, their only foreign market. In some industrial and service sectors, the importance of the EU market is quite impressive. For example, in summer 1997, tourists from the major EU countries (Germany, UK, France and Italy) accounted for roughly one-half of nights spent by foreign guests in Switzerland, that is roughly one-third of total nights registered in Switzerland.

The Swiss economy is also closely linked to the world markets through foreign direct investments (FDI). Switzerland has historically been a major outward investor. On a per capita basis, it has the highest stock of outward investments per person of all OECD member countries reporting stock figures, and ranks seventh in terms of value of its overseas investments. Swiss firms now employ 1.4 million workers outside Switzerland, equivalent to roughly one-third of the Swiss labour force and also similar to the number of foreigners living in Switzerland. During these last few years, the jobs offered by Swiss firms abroad have increased, whereas the number of persons employed in Switzerland has stagnated. Since the 1960s, Swiss FDI has increased dramatically, the stock of Swiss FDI being more than 12 times the amount registered in 1960. Swiss direct investment outflows have remained at a high level since 1988, with very little of the cyclical decline in flows seen in other countries. In 1997, outflows reached a record level with a total of 21 billion Swiss francs. In the UK too, Switzerland is one of the largest investors. As regards acquisitions, in the first half of 1998 it even lay in second place just behind the USA (more than £3 billion!).

As in some other small economies, this outward investment is dominated by a few very large firms. These major Swiss transnational corporations are truly global firms in the sense that their major sales markets are abroad as well as their major production locations. In other words, these firms are increasingly organising or reorganising their cross-border production activities in an efficiency-oriented, integrated fashion, capitalising on the tangible and intangible assets available throughout the corporate system. In the resulting international division of labour within firms, any part of the value-added chain can be located wherever it contributes most to a company's overall performance.

Swiss companies have always been far more international than many of their competitors and they have long since realised that their long-term survival depends on their ability to compete in international markets. The ranking of the Fortune 100 transnational corporations composite index of transnationality shows that four Swiss firms are among the top ten: Nestlé first, Holderbank third, ABB sixth and Roche tenth. (The index of transnationality is calculated as the average of foreign assets to total assets, foreign sales to total sales, and foreign employment to total employment. The data are available for 1995, without Novartis.) Less than 2 per cent of Nestlé's sales are generated in Switzerland and almost 97 per cent of its employees work abroad. Furthermore, the increasing numbers of non-Swiss executives found in Swiss corporate boardrooms is a reflection of the growing international bias of Switzerland's most successful companies.

The evolution of flows since the beginning of the 1990s up to 1996 shows an ever greater divergence between outflows and inflows. Inflows were stagnating, whereas the outflows were very dynamic, especially towards the EU: they rose from 2.7 billion Swiss francs in 1993 to 12.7 billion Swiss francs in 1996. This trend continued in 1997. One should remain cautious as regards the interpretation of these trends. Lack of integration in the EU internal market is certainly an explanation for the dramatic surge in FDI towards the EU. But other factors should be mentioned. One should bear in mind that the relationship between FDI and a country's attractiveness is subtle, resulting from country-specific as well as from firm-specific factors. Apart from the lack of integration in the EU internal markets, globalisation of markets (strategies of firms as regards proximity to the market and so on) as well as overall economic performance in continental Europe and Switzerland are some other factors to be taken into account.

On the other hand FDI inflow into Switzerland has for many years not shown the same dynamism. It remains concentrated in certain service sectors, notably banking and holding companies. From 1992 to 1996, annual inflows have been stagnating, though with a few fluctuations. In particular, the dramatic disinvestment in 1992 is explained by changes in EC tax legislation relating to holding companies. The share of manufacturing in the stock of Swiss inward foreign direct investments amounts to about 15 per cent of the total stock. Interestingly enough, FDI in Switzerland surged in 1997 and was up 80 per cent to 6.4 billion Swiss francs, which is certainly a good sign for the overall conditions offered by Switzerland as a business location.

I would like, thirdly, to turn to these overall conditions, to our competitiveness, to the challenges which we have to overcome on the threshold of the twenty-first century. Globalisation of industry refers to an evolving pattern of cross-border activities of firms involving international investment, trade and collaboration for purposes of sourcing, product development, production and marketing. These international activities enable firms to enter new markets, exploit their technological and organisational advantages, and reduce business costs and risks. Underlying the international expansion of firms, and in part driven by it, are technological advances, the liberalisation of markets and increased mobility of production factors.

Today, firms select their host countries on the basis of their location-specific comparative advantages, which are evaluated by firms according to their likely contribution to the strengthening of their own international competitiveness. Therefore, the aim of each country is to attract value-added activities created by domestic as well as foreign firms by taking action in order to promote the productivity and competitiveness of the firms and resources within its jurisdiction. The competitiveness of a country is determined by its ability to attract or to keep highly mobile factors of production, such as capital and technical competence, within its boundaries.

Long confined to economists, the debate on competitiveness has now burst into the political arena. Countries have joined this global race. Switzerland has also embarked upon what now appears to be a crusade for competitiveness. For the government, it is of tremendous importance to maintain and improve our competitive strengths, while taking action in order to eliminate as far as possible our competitive weaknesses. According to the latest results of studies on international competitiveness, Switzerland is maintaining its position among the ten most competitive countries of the world, and is ranked sixth by the *Global Competitiveness Report 1997* of the World Economic Forum. In this ranking, no European country comes before Switzerland (the UK is ranked seventh). According to the Heritage Foundation Study, Switzerland is among the eight top countries as regards economic freedom, an important factor for economic growth. All these results show a positive basic trend for Switzerland in spite of its rather poor economic record over the 1990s.

What are our main competitive advantages? The answers are manifold: Switzerland offers a central location within Europe's high-tech arena; politically, Switzerland is a stable country; Switzerland offers excellent quality of life, housing conditions and leisure activities; inflation is generally low in Switzerland; interest rates are among the lowest in the world. This is a considerable advantage if capital has to be raised, or if you are running a capital-intensive industry; low tax burden: we have one of the lowest rates of taxation and social security contributions of all industrialised countries.

Other factors are also relevant. For example, the public sector financial position was traditionally strong, though it has deteriorated in recent years. The ratio of consolidated debt is expected to reach 53.2 per cent in 1998. Budget deficit is expected to correspond to 3.5 per cent of GDP in 1998 (not satisfying the Maastricht criterion of 3 per cent of GDP!). Yet one may expect that the consolidation of public finances under the framework of the 'Consolidation Plan 2001' (a constitutional obligation!) will reverse the trend. The level of productivity is quite high. Labour relations in Switzerland, which has one of the longest working weeks in the world with a typical 42 hours, are extremely peaceful and strikes are almost unknown. This is largely due to the 1937 commitment to have collective agreements which require disputes to be settled by arbitration. Switzerland also enjoys a good education system: the workforce is generally highly educated. Entrepreneurs and management are highly experienced in international business, and the language skills of the Swiss are extremely useful in that field, with most people speaking two or more languages, usually including English. According to the *Global Competitiveness Report 1997*, Switzerland ranks in second place for the primary and secondary education system, sixth regarding the quality of its business schools and in first place for the average years of schooling.

In addition, sophisticated communications and transport networks and a highly secure energy supply are available. For example, according to the same *Global Competitiveness Report*, Switzerland ranks first in terms of investment in telecommunications per inhabitant, third for road infrastructures and second for railway infrastructures. Private research and development spending is higher than in most other industrial countries. In fact, private research amounts to 1.9 per cent of GDP. Switzerland ranks behind Sweden (2.7 per cent) and Japan (2 per cent) but before the United States (1.8 per cent). Over the last few years an increasing trend towards 'outsourcing' of research and development has been noticed, reflecting the ever closer co-operation between industry and universities as well as among private firms. Clusters are prevalent in the chemicals industry in Basle, in financial activities in Zurich and Geneva and in the watchmaking industry in the Jura region. Clusters allow for the concentration of skills and of subcontracting enterprises, facilitating the spillover of competence.

The financial sector – banking industry and insurance companies – provides for a favourable business environment and services. Furthermore, the monetary policy of the Swiss National Bank, well known for its determination to maintain price stability, together with one of the world's highest savings rates, provide stable and reliable long-term financing. According to the *Global Competitiveness Report 1997*, Switzerland ranks in first place for the cost of capital, fourth for the adequacy of financial regulation and third for the level of sophistication of financial markets.

Despite this strong competitive potential, Switzerland has during the 1990s somewhat lost part of its attractiveness. Stagnation of economic growth is one of the major concerns. Progression of labour productivity has remained low (in contrast with the good record regarding the level of productivity). But while – according to the

World Competitiveness Yearbook, for instance – we lost some of our competitive advantages in the stagnation period up to 1996, we again improved our ranking in 1997, a move that could reflect the efforts made by the government to improve the economic framework. In fact, the Swiss federal government and cantonal authorities have already taken action and are considering fresh steps in order to strengthen and improve the competitiveness of Switzerland, particularly at the cost level. The main targets of the government action focus on the following issues: the above-mentioned improvement in the public finances; fiscal reforms (in particular to maintain the competitiveness of the Swiss stock exchange); the structural deficiencies in the domestic 'sheltered' sectors of the economy (which often goes along with the cartelisation of the Swiss market), thus preventing market mechanisms and free competition from operating in a sound and efficient way. Indeed, the Swiss export industry is well prepared for the 'global race', whereas the 'sheltered' sectors are not used to functioning in competitive markets; they suffer from discriminatory public procurement practices with cantonal and communal preferences; excessive technical standards limiting competition; slow administrative procedures in some areas (construction permits); limited flexibility in the labour market (for example, limited recognition of qualifications and diplomas among cantons).

Rapid progress has been made in terms of the revitalisation programme in 1995 through the adoption of new laws on cartels (competition law), on the Swiss internal market, on public procurement and on technical barriers to trade, which entered into force in 1996. These new laws aim to improve the competitiveness of Switzerland as a business centre by eliminating or reducing the competitive disadvantages mentioned above. In the field of infrastructure, the reform of postal services, railways and telecommunications is on the way, as well as the liberalisation of the electricity market. Other efforts include agriculture, social security as well as institutional reforms.

A further extremely important field is the international conditions offered. As globalisation of markets continues, one of the major comparative advantages of a nation state is to be able to guarantee to the firms located within its national boundaries effective access to world markets. In fact, the competitiveness of a business location and the market access issue constitute two sides of the same coin. Within this context, Switzerland is facing challenges arising at different levels: the bilateral, the regional, the interregional and the multilateral level.

The primary purpose of the Federal Council's integration policy is to prevent Switzerland's political, economic and cultural isolation within Europe, while at the same time strengthening the Swiss competitive position. Switzerland has had a free trade agreement with the EC since 1972, as well as more than 100 bilateral agreements with the EC. It negotiated, but did not ratify, the European Economic Area (EEA) Treaty – extending the Single European Market to the EFTA countries – which was rejected by 50.3 per cent of the Swiss population and 16 cantons in December 1992. In order to reinforce mutually beneficial relations and alleviate the negative impacts of our non-participation in the Single European Market, the EU and Switzerland are presently negotiating bilateral agreements in the following areas: elimination of technical barriers to trade (mutual recognition of certification and registration of products); public procurement (extension of WTO rules to local communities, including water and energy supplies as well as the railway and telecommunications sectors); research and development (Switzerland seeks full participation in the EU's programmes); free movement of persons (this also covers mutual recognition of diplomas and social security); agricultural products (improved access to markets for agricultural products, for example, liberalisation of the cheese market); land transport and civil aviation (improved access to markets, co-ordinated European transport policy). These negotiations were concluded at expert level, that is with the EC Commission, in the summer of 1998. At the same time, the debate on full EU membership should quickly intensify.

Particular challenges are posed not only by regional integration projects in which we do not participate, but also by the increased co-operation between these, for example, the EU–Mercosur (Argentina, Brazil, Paraguay and Uruguay) framework agreement signed in 1995 or the new 'Transatlantic Partnership' between the EU and the USA aimed at strengthening ties in the areas of trade and security. Tangible achievements in this emerging area of policy activity are only beginning to take shape, but questions about what the interregional dynamic will mean for Switzerland are increasingly relevant. Thus Swiss firms in a regional union market could face discrimination compared to external firms located in another union, enjoying preferential agreement with the union in question. Here also, priority has to be given to the strengthening of our links with those regional unions and their member states. In 1997, Switzerland held bilateral talks with the USA on the prospects of a Mutual Recognition Agreement (MRA) between the two countries; an MRA is currently under negotiation with Canada as well as a free trade agreement between Canada and EFTA.

At the global multilateral level, the strengthening of WTO rules in order to prevent a competitive disadvantage for Swiss firms is also a priority. So for Switzerland the conclusion of the WTO negotiations on telecommunications in February 1997 and on financial services in December 1997 represented extremely important steps. Switzerland supports actions taken in order to ensure the dynamic development of a truly universal, fully functional trading system responsive to the needs of small and large trading nations alike. Consolidation of the results achieved to date, continued attention to a range of issues which have long figured on the multinational agenda and progress on emerging trade issues are all relevant in this context.

I am aware that I have by no means mentioned, let alone shed light on, all the important factors which will be decisive for the success of the Swiss economy in the coming century. For instance, one should undoubtedly raise the question of whether Switzerland's political structures are still adequate with regard to overcoming the economic challenges. Or one should look in detail at the structures of individual sectors and their productivity and so on. However, that would be going too far here, and I would not be the right person for this task.

However, I cannot avoid one last topic, that is, the effects of the euro and European Monetary Union (EMU) on the Swiss economy. EMU represents a huge challenge for Switzerland in particular, as an outsider. On the one hand our enterprises, especially those which are internationally active, also benefit from the advantages of the single currency. On the other, they too are exposed to more vigorous competition – with its watchwords of price transparency and increased efficiency. In addition, there are uncertainties on the monetary side. If the European currency lacks stability, we can expect higher demand for Swiss francs, and hence an increase in value. The volatility of the franc could also increase as there are few sound alternative currencies to the euro, with the Swiss franc being the smallest. From this point of view in particular, we are especially interested in the future of the British pound. Nevertheless, the single currency of our most important trade partners will undoubtedly strengthen the integration of the Swiss economy in the European area. The linking of the Swiss financial sector to the euro area will be reinforced by Switzerland's access to the European payments system and the co-operation of the Swiss stock market with stock markets in the EMU.

I am convinced that EMU will promote the concentration of enterprises in the sphere of small and medium-sized enterprises in Switzerland as well, because it will bring about a reduction in costs. But as in the past, our economy will also manage to build up its strength under pressure from outside. As regards productivity in this context, top-quality services are necessary as well as innovative product ideas, raising the quality of consultancy and services, correctly adapted and optimised financial management, accounting, controls and so on. While the financial markets sector seems to be well equipped, surveys in the trade and tourism sector reveal that this still lags behind somewhat. But high demands are placed on the state as well, for it is necessary to optimise the advantages of the country as a business location and to provide even better overall conditions for enterprises. I will just briefly mention the fields of tax, salaries and social contributions, and monetary policy. At present, in the event of strong upward pressure on the franc the Swiss National Bank seems to favour a strategy of expanding the money supply (involving the danger of inflation) over linking the franc to the euro (involving the rapid loss of our interest rate advantage).

I hope that my comments, which are not comprehensive and which have tended perhaps inevitably to oversimplify the issues, have conveyed to you a picture of the current position of the Swiss economy and the challenges which confront it on the threshold of the twenty-first century.

8
Redefining Swiss Relations with Europe

Clive H. Church

Traditionally, scholars have distinguished between internal and external politics and seen them as largely separate. But analysis of both the Swiss economy and of constitutional change, shows that Swiss domestic politics are closely related to outside developments. In fact it is very much the case that Swiss external policy, whether linked to Europe or beyond, is affected by internal constraints. Indeed, it has been said that Switzerland does not have a foreign policy, only a domestic policy aimed at preventing external events from disturbing the internal balance and status quo. This may be an exaggeration but it does highlight a key element of Switzerland's relations with Europe. One of the ironies in the celebrations of the 150th anniversary of a small state, at the geographical heart of Europe, and of very European characteristics, is that Switzerland is surprisingly uncertain about its political position in the world, a question which one would expect to have been long since resolved. Yet Switzerland is still debating the next stage of its relations with the European institutions, not to mention worrying about its standing in the wider world. Hence one of its tasks as it faces the new millennium is to redefine its relations with Europe.

However, whereas in the past there seemed to be a series of options open to Switzerland, this no longer seems to be the case. The choice seems to have narrowed to membership of the EU or some variant of the bilateral status quo. And the redefinition will, ultimately, have to be made by the Swiss people themselves. So, rather as in the United Kingdom, redefining Swiss relations with Europe is not so much a matter of identifying new courses of action but of eliminating impractical alternatives and resolving internal disputes about them. Making this clear requires analysing the present situation of Swiss relations with the Union and why many people think that this constitutes a problem, both in terms of Switzerland's economic position and its own internal divisions. Equally it means looking at how and why the present situation has come about through long and difficult negotiations, constrained both by internal reticence and external pressures. Finally it needs consideration of what possibilities there are for a redefinition of Swiss relations with Europe. And, if the country chooses to stay outside the Union, how will it fare at the beginning of the new millennium and its second 150 years?

The answer has to be that there is more chance of Switzerland moving towards membership now than in recent years. However, the internal obstacles remain. As a result the situation is balanced on a knife edge so that, whatever is decided, relations with Europe may remain problematic. And this is not untypical of the uncertainties with which the Swiss celebrate their 150th anniversary, uncertainties which are intimately linked to the political system created since 1848 and the political culture to which it has given rise.

Switzerland and Europe today

Of all West European countries Switzerland is the one which belongs to the fewest institutions, even if it is heavily engaged in Europe in other ways. And attempts to draw closer to the EU have made only slow and uncertain progress. For some all this is a major problem politically and economically. Others see it as a major benefit and justification of Swiss traditions, and something which has not affected the country's robust economic health. For much of the postwar period Switzerland has tended to reject formal membership of many of the regional and global institutions to which most of her neighbours belong. The decision to do so has been endorsed by the Swiss population on a number of occasions. Yet, at the same time, the country has been very fully involved in the economic and technical life of such organisations and their member states. And, in the past, this unusual stance seemed to work pretty well.

In more recent years there have been pressures, both governmental and popular, for more structured relationships with international organisations. As a result Switzerland is considering new relationships with the EU. However, achieving this has not proved easy. Moreover, for the first time, the country is finding itself exposed to worldwide criticism of a largely new kind, because of some of its alleged wartime activities. Equally, the risk management skills of its banks have come under open attack. Being in the public eye is not something the Swiss really enjoy. In other words, the country finds itself in a new kind of isolation.

In institutional terms, therefore, Switzerland is not a full member of the United Nations. It is only an observer, a status somewhat less than that now enjoyed by the Palestine Liberation Organisation. And a proposal to join was crushingly defeated in 1986. However, it has now joined the IMF and the World Bank. Within Europe, the Swiss are active members of bodies such as the Council of Europe and the CSCE. They are also involved in the NATO Partnership for Peace. But they remain outside the European Union and the European Economic Area. Their application to join the former, which is often overlooked as a glance at the British government's document on the 1996 IGC shows, has been frozen since early 1993.

The government did this following the narrow refusal by the people on 6 December 1992 to ratify the EEA Treaty. This left Switzerland as the only member of the European Free Trade Association not in the EEA. Even Liechtenstein, with whom it has had an economic and monetary union since 1922, chose to go the other way, forcing a renegotiation of the accords between the two states. In this, Switzerland differed from Norway, the other major Western state not to pursue EU membership. And the political profiles and economic interests of the two countries are sufficiently different to prevent the close alliance that some thought possible.

However, just as Switzerland is fully involved in many of the UN's technical agencies, so the country is involved in many EU programmes. In fact, until recently the Swiss had more technical agreements with the Community than any other state. One of these is an agreement on Alpine transit facilities, committing the Swiss to build base line rail tunnels under the mountains. This was signed when the EEA deal was initialled in 1991 although it was complicated by the 1994 Alpine Initiative *votation* which requires all transalpine traffic to go by rail after 2004.

Even more striking is Swiss involvement in the EU economy. Not merely do 78.8 per cent of its imports come from the EU and

60.8 per cent of its exports go there, but it is the second largest investor in the EU, nearly half its direct investment flowing there. Equally, it provides work in Switzerland (and abroad) for large numbers of EU citizens. And, since 1994, the country has been seeking to consolidate this by negotiating a series of major bilateral accords, designed to provide an equivalent to key provisions in the EEA Agreement. Some related minor deals, often with individual countries, including one on customs fraud, were concluded ahead of the conclusion of talks in December 1998.

Furthermore, not only has the application for EU membership never been withdrawn, but the aim of joining has been reasserted by the government with the tacit support of the population. Thus a right-wing initiative which would have made all negotiations with the EU, including the bilateral talks, dependent on a positive referendum decision, was emphatically rejected in June 1997. Immediately after this an initiative calling for a second vote on the EEA was withdrawn because it was an irrelevance, given both the eclipse of the EEA and the success of a later initiative, 'Yes to Europe', which calls for immediate entry negotiations. Launched in February 1995 and largely ignored by business, this did, finally on 30 July 1996, get enough signatures to force a referendum.

These referenda are symbolic of the divisive political effects the EEA vote has had at home. In 1992 the country was virtually split down the middle along a number of cleavage lines, including those between French and German speakers. Rather as in Britain, two cultures, insular and traditional on the one hand, and progressive and outward looking on the other, have been in conflict. The 1992 vote also raised concerns about both national cohesion and confidence in the country's government and institutions. The European issue also helped to polarise opinion in the 1995 General Elections, so there is major political uncertainty about the way forward.

However, early in the summer of 1998, the government, in line with President Cotti's call for 1998 to be the 'Swiss Year of Europe', responded to the 'Yes' initiative by proposing a decree which would offer parliamentary approval for a policy of taking part in integration. It promised that, 'to this end', the country 'shall endeavour to become a member of the European Union'. There is also a commitment to active preparation for entry, the Federal Council being left to judge, in the light of the bilaterals and reactions to their promised report, when to open talks. And opinion polls suggest support for entry is now growing, while the Christian Democratic Party and pro-European movements have come out in favour of rapid entry. Yet paradoxically, at the time the country thus began to emerge from its European isolation, it has found itself exposed to new pressures from outside. Thus there has been criticism of its refusal to create a force of 'blue helmets' to aid the UN. Equally its asylum policy and its decision to deport unsuccessful applicants from Bosnia and Kosovo back to their homelands have both come under fire. More importantly, the running crisis over Nazi gold led to threats of boycotts and sanctions against Swiss financial and commercial interests in the United States. These have now apparently been averted thanks to a global deal, negotiated with the banks in New York in August 1998. But the incessant attacks from the World Jewish Congress and others to secure a deal has had a dire effect on the country's image and revealed that it no longer enjoyed the goodwill it had assumed. And its friends and allies turned out to be less supportive than might have been hoped. So public opinion has been even more disorientated about the way forward in external policy.

To what extent these difficulties with Europe have harmed Switzerland is a subject of great internal debate. For many, they have been a real problem, politically and economically. Politically, such difficulties have raised the spectre of international isolation. Economically, things have also become difficult in a number of ways.

To begin with, in this view, Switzerland has become dangerously marginalised in Europe. With the entry of the EFTA countries into the EU, Switzerland is left on its own, on the wrong side of the Schengen barrier and seen as the new centre of crime, notably cigarette smuggling. This apartness is very much brought home to the Swiss both when they travel in Europe, and find themselves both forced to queue with the rest of the world at airports rather than using faster European channels and to try and obtain work permits for EU countries. Similarly, the country has found itself cut off from some European-wide programmes because it is not in the EU. All this can be seen as very demeaning to Swiss pride and self-esteem. There is also a feeling that the country is being held to ransom by an inward-looking minority. Many people have therefore started to worry about the domestic Swiss decision-making process and its lack of adaptability to new challenges.

Secondly, in terms of negotiations it is at a disadvantage. The bilateral experience has shown that it is harder for one small state on its own to get the EU to agree terms than for a group of countries. This is particularly so for Switzerland because the EU is able to use Swiss direct democracy against the Swiss and prevent it from choosing those elements most favourable to it. In any case, the bilaterals do not offer anything in the way of shared decision-making. Equally bodies such as the Council of Europe and the European Conference of Ministers of Transport, which Switzerland might expect to use to balance its exclusion, have lost much of their importance with the various moves to enlargement of the EU. Even EFTA has now largely moved to Brussels from Geneva. Official policy is clear that only through membership can co-decision be achieved. Hence the bilateral road is seen as only a short-term solution.

This reflects the fact that, thirdly, the Swiss very often have to adjust to European rules without being able to share in making them. Getting information about what is coming is harder for them than others. Moreover, following the 1992 *votation*, the government has had to adapt Swiss laws to meet European standards and practices whether it wanted to or not. As it is, Swiss ways are not always very open and competitive and Europeanisation is a way of revitalising them. Firms like Holderbank are still being fined for breaking EU cartel laws for instance. Swiss institutions have also been forced to adjust in varying ways. Thus the cantons themselves have had to get involved in European matters.

Economically, there are also problems, especially as the Asian crisis has threatened the country's second largest market. Firstly, by being outside the Single Market, Swiss firms face more administrative hurdles than their competitors. They have to undergo more administrative formalities (including those over rules of origin and at customs inspections) which means longer delivery times. They can also face higher costs, for instance when bidding for contracts under EU public procurement rules. Complaints about EU discrimination have almost doubled since 1994. In transport, Swissair, which remains largely state owned, has found itself excluded from the more open market emerging in the Union, an exclusion symbolised by its problems with the new airport arrangements in Milan. All this has cost it some 200 million francs a year and has forced it to centralise on Zurich, to the detriment of Geneva, much to the annoyance of French speakers who are also seeing their chances of mobility declining.

At the same time, many Swiss firms have adjusted their strategies because they are outside the Single Market. Firms like Sulzer, Roche and Alusuisse have closed facilities in Switzerland and transferred production to EU countries. This is even true of the Swatchmobile project. Inward investment has declined, often to the advantage of countries like Austria, while Swiss outward investment has soared. Overall, it is reckoned that 50 000 jobs have been cut in Switzerland while 100 000 have been created outside, often in the EU. Machines and textiles have been worst hit by all this and even the banks are uneasy.

Lastly, because the country is outside the EU it has been painfully attractive to footloose capital funds. This has pushed up the value of the franc, with unfortunate effects on competitiveness, nowhere more so than in the tourist industry which has suffered its worst downturn in generations. Uncertainties over EMU threaten to repeat the dose as well as causing new problems for the financial services. Many firms will have to invoice in euros and absorb the resulting exchange losses. Switzerland is also under pressure to introduce a new 'withholding' tax on bank deposits to help the EU. All of this has, for some, depressed GDP growth and jobs, which has not helped an economy which, in the mid-1990s, experienced its largest downturn since 1945.

On the other hand, many vociferous opponents of closer relations with the Union deny most of this. They argue that the country has not merely been unscathed but may even have been strengthened by what has happened, both politically and, especially, economically. None of the plagues forecast at the time of the rejection of the EEA has come true. Hence, for them, the real danger is continuing to think in terms of entry to the EU because it is better that Switzerland should go it alone. This *Alleingang* option is, for them, not necessarily isolationist.

In political terms they would argue that far from being demeaning, the decision to stay out has preserved Swiss national traditions, pride and interest. It has shown that the Swiss people make their own decisions and will not be kicked around by Swiss Europhiles, let alone by Eurocrats. This has reinforced the effectiveness of direct democracy. Equally the country has stayed united and may even have become more democratic because the government has been forced to rein back its Euro enthusiasm and take more notice of parliament and people, even if it has not actually withdrawn its application for membership.

Externally, they would doubt that the country really needs to bother with influencing the EU, given its favourable balance of trade with Switzerland. Certainly they question whether the bilaterals were really necessary, and may challenge the deal if they think it has given too much away as, in their view, negotiations by the present establishment usually do. In any case they believe there is no hurry because 'time is on our side'. Indeed, if there are technical difficulties in trade and trade legislation then these can best be solved through the WTO.

No value at all is placed on the EEA with its 'colonial laws'. These are seen as being as profoundly inimical as any other form of integration to what is a more democratic system than that found anywhere else in Europe. And, in any case, in so far as the economy needs revitalising, this can be done domestically just as easily and effectively as by outside stimulus, notably by reducing social spending. The recent consolidation of the two big banks might suggest that this is already happening. Moreover, maintaining present policies on Europe may do away with the need to build costly new tunnels, while also aiding the environment.

In economic terms, as this implies, their view is that Switzerland has done very well despite the general slump, and certainly much better than EEA and EU countries. Hence Switzerland remains the richest country in the world. Its research and development facilities are world-rated, its competitiveness is high, and its trade is in surplus. In terms of inflation, debt and deficit the country is more able than most EU countries to meet the Maastricht convergence criteria, should it ever wish to do so. Above all they point to its enviable unemployment rates, even after their recent surge, and despite paying remarkably high wages.

They would see the continuing attractiveness of Switzerland as a safe haven as a considerable asset, and one which is likely to continue. This is especially so given that the country is a 'low interest rate island'. Equally, its stock exchange is healthy and wired into wider European networks. This means that investment from Germany is continuing and more companies generally are setting up in Switzerland.

All in all Switzerland is in far better shape than her EU rivals and is likely to remain so if it avoids getting sucked into the costly interventionism of Brussels. If there are problems they are products of structural weakness and not of exclusion from the EEA. In other words, beyond an acceptance that Switzerland is not in either the EEA or the EU, there is virtually no agreement between the two sides about Switzerland's actual position and prospects.

The background

The next question is how did Switzerland find itself in this situation of being outside the main institutions and experiencing such disagreement about joining them? And why was this? The answers seem to be mainly that there are, as has already become clear, very considerable domestic political resistances to a more Euro-friendly policy. Equally, there have also been many outside obstacles along the road to negotiations with the EU.

In the past the Swiss have sought to ensure that they gain as much economic advantage from European integration as is possible without getting sucked in politically, to the detriment of their historic principle of neutrality. Hence, after the slow adjustment to bodies like the Council of Europe there came the encouragement to create EFTA. When this ceased to be a meaningful alternative to the EC, it was used as a means of managing small states' relations with the EU. As a result a free-trade deal was negotiated in 1972 which gave free access to the Common Market for Swiss industrial goods. This was then built on pragmatically through a whole series of technical co-operation agreements. These led the Swiss to think of themselves as 'quasi-members' of the EC.

However, this was not really the case and Swiss officials became increasingly aware that they were unable to influence the developments that increasingly affected them. Hence they looked for a third way which would give them such leverage while ensuring that they would not get sucked into membership. They thought that this 'third way' might be found in the 1984 Luxembourg agreements between the EC and EFTA. But this proved not to be the case thanks to the new dynamism of the EC. The latter's concentration on enlargement, the 1992 project and institutional reform meant that it either paid little attention to EFTA or insisted that its own interests came first.

This, along with developments in Eastern Europe, forced the government to rethink its position. Hence from the late 1980s a new, and more rounded, foreign policy paradigm emerged. This involved military reform, a relaxing of neutrality, which was seen as compatible with closer relations with Brussels, and a new line on European relations. After some hesitation the Swiss committed themselves to the Delors initiative of January 1989 which was, eventually, to lead to the EEA. Negotiations on this were long and difficult and in the end led to something which the Swiss negotiators felt would not be compatible with national dignity over the long term. Adjustments made to the deal in the light of objections by the European Court of Justice reinforced this feeling. Hence the somewhat precipitate move to apply for membership in May 1992, an application motivated mainly by the belief that only inside the Community could the country really defend its own interests. This reflected the fact that all the other EFTA countries were applying for membership, making the EEA seem even less attractive as a long-term solution to the European question. It was also a decision encouraged by a misreading of public opinion after the clear approval of Swiss membership of the World Bank and the International Monetary Fund. However, it was to prove a paradigm too far for public opinion as became clear on 6 December.

Thereafter the Swiss sought to find a stop-gap solution through bilateral negotiations. As government reports in February and November of 1993 made clear, this was the only possible line of approach open and had to have priority, even though entry remained the long-term goal. However, these were to prove a long drawn out and up and down affair. And very often the Swiss seem to have made most concessions. Hence the talks have satisfied neither opponents nor supporters of closer relations with the EU.

Though the idea of a bilateral approach was floated early in 1993, not until the autumn of that year was agreement reached to negotiate, and then on a narrower front than the Swiss wanted. But before they could really start, the Alpine Initiative vote threw a further spanner in the works. Although the necessary clarification that the results of the negotiations could be implemented in a way which was neither discriminatory nor out of line with the rest of the emerging deal was eventually provided, meaningful talks were effectively delayed until early 1995. Even then they did not make much progress and, by the autumn, there was talk of deadlock despite new concessions by the Swiss. Hence an interim government *Report on Integration*, published in March 1995, could do no more than stress the importance of getting a bilateral deal. A further stage began in February 1996 but the Community was slow to respond to new Swiss offers that spring. And, despite talk of people working like galley slaves to get a deal there seems to have been more deadlock than progress. Talk of a breakthrough having been made, as in May 1996 and January 1997, proved somewhat exaggerated. So, although some progress was made, many details remained unsolved.

Things got worse as 1997 went by, and come May, the talks were in full crisis thanks to the cancellation of an expected meeting of the Transport Council. However, they were never broken off and, despite a war of nerves in the autumn, when a further Council meeting was called off, a crucial breakthrough on transport was eventually made at Kloten Airport in Zurich on 23 January 1998. This owed much to a new Swiss offer on 10 October and to Neil Kinnock's promptings. It seemed to have broken the crucial logjam. Even so things still went slowly. A Council meeting in March noted that progress had been made and did not reject it. But, as Germany remained unconvinced, a formal deal could not be struck. Hence thought was given by the Swiss to leaving out the two transport questions altogether. So it proved hard to build on the Kloten deal until mid-June when the technical details in the remaining dossiers were finally, and unexpectedly, agreed.

Yet doubts remained and while, at first, it was hoped this was a mere pause pending the German election, such hopes were again called into question. There was even some fear, both of the talks being blocked and of an ultimate solution not coming until the spring of 1999, during the German Presidency. Equally, the shadow of the Swiss *votations* on the remaining financial issues related to the transit accords raised further doubts. It all suggested that the saga might last for far more than the anticipated six years.

To a large extent these difficulties have their roots in Swiss domestic politics. In fact the importance of Swiss domestic concerns goes well beyond the role that writers like Kelstrup and Puttnam see them playing. As already suggested, internal constraints often play the pre-eminent part in the making of Swiss foreign policy. Hence there is little doubt that what now constrains Swiss policy on Europe most are a series of internal factors. These include the nature of mainstream political culture, with its focus on institutions of direct democracy; the surprising lack of trust in the government; and the fact that opponents of integration have been better able to utilise the changing nature of Swiss politics to get their message across. All this has severely impeded the government.

Whereas after the last war questions of neutrality played a major part in persuading Swiss governments not to apply for membership in the UN, the Council of Europe and the EEC, with the passage of time the nature and significance of neutrality have changed. Originally a tool to prevent the country from getting embroiled in external conflicts which might threaten national cohesion, neutrality has become a value in itself. In fact, it got caught up in a broader political culture, sometimes nicknamed 'Swissitude'. Because of the country's apparent ability to resist Nazi pressures through its own devices many people came to believe that the Swiss systems in culture, economics and politics, both internal and external, were the secret of their success. Therefore any changes to them were threatening and unwise, especially given the dangers of which many Swiss remained fearful, a response often likened to the *Igelstellung* of the Second World War years. So change as such, rather than any technical developments inside neutrality, became a problem.

Increasingly, direct democracy assumed the key role in this new Swiss political culture. It was the system of initiatives and challenges which allowed the Swiss to control their own destiny and which marked them off from other, less convincing, representative democracies. Joining 'Europe', it was argued, would curtail such rights and hence undermine the foundation of national identity and self-determination. Moreover, a significant fact is that, from 1977, acceding to the Community would have to be approved by a referendum. Such views were not necessarily those of the majority, and were often contested. And, in many circumstances, they might not have mattered because the government would have been able to persuade the electorate to approve membership as being in the country's best interests. Unfortunately, at the time the key votes were taken, two other factors intervened.

To begin with, the electorate experienced a major loss of confidence in the government. Levels of trust fell from 57 to 38 per cent between 1988 and 1992. This was due to a number of factors: the way the government failed to alter course after the rejection of UN entry; the revelations (following the resignation of the first woman cabinet minister for lying to parliament) that the government had been keeping secret files on one in six of the population, and the feeling that the establishment was too closely linked to big business. Hence the biggest single indicator of a 'No' vote in December 1992 was lack of trust. The fact that the government wanted entry effectively damned the idea in many people's eyes, especially after the government had spent so long sniping at Brussels. The opposition was thus able to turn the Federal Council's own words against it and create a very divisive impression of betrayal.

What made things worse for the supporters of integration was that opposition to the EEA was far better organised and more effective than the government case. Led by Christoph Blocher of the Swiss People's Party (SVP), and working mainly through his isolationist movement, the Association for a Neutral and Independent Switzerland (AUNS), the 'No' campaign was far better adjusted to the new media-dominated world of Swiss politics. Such opposition had emerged at the time of the UN *votation* but had become increasingly Eurosceptic. It was also able to draw on the way that critical German-speaking conservatives, the so-called *Neinsager*, are more likely to vote than others. And their votes gain additional significance from the fact that many *votations* require a double majority of citizens and cantons, and the cantonal balance is tipped in favour of small, traditionalist German-speaking Alpine cantons.

In any case, the opposition was well organised and financed. Hence it was able to use previous government criticisms of the EEA in a very effective, if emotive, campaign. It was also able to prevent the government outspending it on the grounds that the rules did not allow it to take one side. This reflected a feeling that government was there to administer and not to 'give a lead'. And, as most ministers are chosen for their collegial appeal, they do not include the kind of political bruisers like Prescott and Clarke who would be able to stand up to the likes of Blocher. Moreover, the 'Yes' campaign was too rational and cautious. It failed to win over floating voters, let alone those committed to a go-it-alone policy. Many of these were rural and small business interests which would lose from any lowering of frontier barriers in a way that big, export-orientated firms would not. Equally, many habitual non-voters turned out to vote against the EEA, reflecting a selective tendency for electors to concern themselves mainly with foreign policy issues with internal implications.

The loss of the 1992 *votation* was a terrible shock to the Federal Council. Hence it immediately backtracked. It reverted to the normal Swiss tradition of trying to build up an all-embracing coalition, something which was almost impossible in the new polarised atmosphere. Hence the government suffered further signal defeats on foreign policy matters, notably when environmental issues were brought into play in 1994. This reflected the continuing strength of anti-EU feelings, orchestrated by AUNS which has often booed pro-European ministers and, from April 1996, moved beyond warning against bilateral deals which essentially replicate the EEA to threatening a referendum challenge come what may. In December 1997 Blocher sent an open letter to all households in the country setting out his case that staying out of the EEA had done the country no harm at all. Attempts by the Social Democrats, pro-European interests and business to keep the European flag flying have been much less effective, perhaps reflecting the fact that many mainstream politicians also had doubts of their own.

So, while the government's basic policy has remained unchanged, it has had to be careful not to flaunt its hopes for entry. This means essentially that while seeking an interim bilateral deal, the Federal Council has, in effect, been forced to wait until public opinion really comes round to their way of thinking. In the absence of an effective information policy, of wholehearted support from the mainline parties and of certainty about the approval of the bilaterals, this has not yet really happened.

However, the difficulties do not only lie in the caution forced on Swiss negotiators by the post-1992 internal political context. Such internal difficulties have interacted with problems caused by the EU itself. The latter thus limited the range of the bilaterals, reacted badly to Swiss toughness and showed itself to be both slow and divided. Equally, the fact that the Union was very aware that agreement is subject to ratification by the hostile and unreliable Swiss electorate further complicated matters. Hence the EU's own interests and reservations encouraged a kind of brinkmanship right up to the very last moment.

Certainly, the bilateral talks did not extend as far as the Swiss had wanted since the Community wanted a balanced package of benefit to both sides and not simply those which would favour the Swiss. In the end they covered six main areas, one of which, transport, was

clearly divided into land and air. The easy dossiers were public procurement, where the Swiss sought wider access while allowing EU
firms to bid for local government contracts; non-tariff barriers, where
the Swiss wanted to be able to certify their own goods rather than
submitting to EU scrutiny; and research and development, where
the Swiss sought to buy full access in the running and management
of Community programmes. Agriculture posed more problems since
while the authorities were willing to reduce tariffs and quotas, as the
EC wanted, Swiss peasants were not happy about giving reciprocal
rights to EU produce.

However, the real difficulties were the free movement of labour
and transport. On the first the Community really wanted the Swiss
to apply the complete freedom of movement found in the Single
Market, rather than the restrictive and complicated series of categories
of work permit adopted by the Swiss. But this touched a Swiss nerve
about excessive immigration. In transport, the negotiations really
called into question the essence of Swiss transport policy, since the
Community wanted the Swiss to do away with their bans on heavy
lorries and to make only a minimal charge for traversing the Alps.
Partly in compensation Switzerland sought the freedom for its airlines
and haulage firms to be allowed to provide services anywhere in the
EU, the so-called right of *cabotage*, and not just between Switzerland
and a given EU centre.

Not surprisingly, many Swiss interest groups have been exercised by
these negotiations. Some, like Swissair, have pushed for a deal. Others,
like environmentalists and the Alpine cantons, have been very resist-
ant to any change in the country's strict controls on lorries over
28 tonnes. Swiss transport concerns have been somewhat divided, as
have farming interests. And many people, including the anti-European
forces, have been violently opposed to allowing free movement
because of what this could do to the delicate balance of Swiss society.
All this has added to the government's strategic caution about giving
too much away to Europe and made it, as is normally the case, a
tough negotiator.

This stance has sometimes proved counter-productive. Thus the
Union was at first uncertain about the wisdom of engaging in bilateral
talks in such circumstances. For President Klestil of Austria, for
example, these were not the way to solve the 'Swiss problem'. They
were seen as cumbersome and basically a sop to the Swiss. Hence,

while there was sympathy in principle, there has not always been the political will, even in largely supportive countries like Austria and Germany, to overcome technical problems and the competing pressures of their own interest groups. Moreover, having sought such talks, the EU has often felt the Swiss to be surprisingly slow and inflexible in negotiating. Thus it felt that both the Alpine Initiative and the refusal to grant equal rights to EU workers in Switzerland were discriminatory. There were even threats of countermeasures to the former. There was also a great deal of opposition to the level of charges which the Swiss wanted to levy on transit across the Alps and it took a long time before these were talked down to a point where they became acceptable.

In any case, the EU has not been united on the substantive issues and so often failed to support the Commission's line. Its own economic negotiating cycles were also long drawn out. Moreover, while some states were willing to see a rapid deal struck, others felt their concerns were not sufficiently protected. Thus France wanted more access to Swiss agricultural markets, the Italians and Germans were particularly opposed to any increase in transit charges, and the Iberian states wanted better treatment for their many workers in Switzerland. Towards the end of the negotiations the Austrians also objected to the Swiss, as a non-member country, enjoying a better deal than they had secured. As a result the Swiss sometimes saw the EU as being intransigent and unwilling to meet them halfway, if not of being unwilling to enter into meaningful talks at all. They were also unhappy that the whole deal had been treated as a package even though it was not in a single document. The assumption of the EU had always been that if one element of the package was rejected in the negotiations, the other elements would also lapse. While this is not absolutely certain, the possibility put great pressure on the Swiss since they were the ones who most keenly wanted a deal, for both internal and general reasons.

These problems on the EU side continued right up to the very last minute of the negotiations. Getting a deal after the German elections proved as arduous and uncertain as previous stages in the negotiations. Talk of postponement into the New Year was not unknown. This was because, despite encouragement from Robin Cook, helpful votes in Switzerland and pressure from the General Affairs Council and the Swiss authorities, there was continuing resistance among some states, even though the new Social Democratic government in Germany did prove more helpful than Helmut Kohl's administration. Although, following a new mandate from the General Affairs Council to the Commission, a revised transport agreement was concluded by Kinnock and Leuenberger on 1 December, this was not the end of the story. Hence, the Swiss had to make further concessions in the endgame in December 1998. For while Swiss ministers were on standby in Berne to come and approve the package, it ran into further trouble among the EU foreign ministers, then gathering to prepare the Vienna Summit. French resistance to granting concessions to Swissair and the use of the term 'champagne' by some Vaudois wine producers were among the last-minute obstacles. Side agreements on asylum and combating fraud did, however, emerge.

In the end, the Swiss gave way on the champagne issue in order to aid Swissair. The package went back to COREPER for solution by written procedure where some states were recalcitrant for a while. And, at the last moment, the Portuguese dug their heels in over the timing of concessions on free movement and tariff-based competition with port wine. Their objections were not withdrawn until the night of Thursday 10 December, allowing the Swiss President and the Minister of Economics to come to Vienna to seal the agreement. The full texts were initialled in late January 1999, signed at the end of March and, assuming ratification by the Swiss, the European Parliament and the Member States, will start to come into effect on 1 January 2001. Not all of its provisions will come into immediate operation.

The final deal covered all seven aspects of the negotiations and, thanks to the inaptly named 'guillotine' clause, has to stand or fall as a single package. In public procurement there will be mutual liberalisation and the Swiss will create their own Surveillance Authority and allow equal rights of appeal to those available in the EU. The deal will now include communes as well as cantonal levels and above. And it will extend to transport and communications. In research and development the Swiss will get full rights of access thanks to a payment into the EC's programmes funds of some 600 million francs over five years. There will also be mutual recognition of standards and norms as a way of dealing with non-tariff barriers to trade. In agriculture, EU products will get preferential access, eventually even to the Swiss cheese market, thanks to a range of tariff cuts, while Switzerland will also harmonise relevant legislation.

On the thorny subject of free movement there will be a five-year transition period after which the right of establishment will come into effect. Switzerland will also, over seven years, phase out its quotas on foreign workers where existing EU residents are concerned. Preferential conditions and consideration for Swiss workers will also be removed. Controversially, equal rights of access to social security allowances will be provided even for short-term workers. By the end of 12 years all barriers to free movement will be removed, though there will be safeguards against any sudden mass influxes.

Where land transport is concerned there will be a quota of 40-tonne lorries until full liberalisation is achieved in 2005. By then lorries will be charged for crossing the Alps. The amount levied, which will depend on weight, tendency to pollute and the distance travelled, will reach a maximum of 320–330 francs in 2006–7. This, it is hoped, will encourage lorries to go by rail using the new base tunnels which should be open by then. Equally Swiss hauliers will get rights of *cabotage* in the EU.

In the skies the deal will allow Swissair to benefit from the third and fourth freedoms which allow *cabotage* at once, while the fifth and seventh freedoms, which permit prolongation flights between EU countries, will come in later. Negotiations on the eighth freedom – to provide internal services in EU countries – are due to take place after five years. The Swiss will also adjust their technical and competition rules in the field.

Towards the future?

Having eventually secured this bilateral deal, almost six years to the day after the EEA was rejected, the Swiss still have further obstacles to overcome in redefining their relations with Europe. One of these is whether the bilaterals are self-sufficient or are merely a transitional preliminary to membership. The government's chances of moving on to reactivating its application for membership, in fact depend on resolving this question. If the bilaterals have helped to continue the process of eliminating alternatives to membership, it is not clear that people are willing to take the next step and endorse membership. And if the package is not ratified, or if the application fails, then relations will remain divisive and problematical. This points to the continuing uncertainties facing Switzerland in the new millennium.

The first question now facing the Swiss elite is how, having concluded a bilateral deal, can it actually be delivered? The text was formally agreed at the end of March 1999. The European parliament will look at the package in the autumn of 1999 after which it will go to national parliaments for ratification. While the latter are unlikely to block it, there must be questions as to whether the Federal Council can sell the package as a whole to the Swiss electorate. At present the auspices are relatively good. After all, on 27 September 1998, the Swiss voted conclusively to accept the principle of taxing lorries in transit according to weight and distance and then, on 29 November, they agreed by 63.6 to 36.4 per cent (admittedly on a low turnout) to approve the financing of proposed sub-Alpine tunnels. This showed that the population, urged on by pro-European forces, was willing to back the Federal Council against its own transport lobby and the forces of anti-Europeanism. Both had objected to the proposals which are crucial to the Kloten solution. The *votations* removed some technical and political threats to a solution and helped, as already noted, to give the Swiss enough credibility to finalise the bilateral agreements.

However, although public opinion has generally accepted the idea of bilateral deals, the fact that Switzerland can be seen as having given way on free movement and transit charges will be used by the opposition to change minds. Moreover, it can also seize on the fact that the package will cost the country some 3.5 billion francs, thanks in part to the concessions on social security eligibility. The far right has already announced that it will challenge the package at referendum and the SVP may support this. Some other internal interests may also still feel that they get too little out of the deal. This demands a firm campaign by the government. However, too aggressive selling by the government could be counter-productive. The government will hope to convince its citizens that its strategy and tactics are correct through a series of reports it is due to produce in the near future: on the implications of membership, on the balance sheet of the bilateral approach, and on the implementation of the alternative to the 'Yes to Europe' initiative. Initial hints suggest that the first report is likely to be heavily technical while trying to show that EU entry is both a better solution than either the bilaterals or the EEA. And it will be portrayed as one which will not overtax the Swiss. Whether this will address the underlying fears about Swiss identity remains to be seen.

In any case, the government, according to recent accounts, finds itself caught in a dilemma. If it makes too much of the bilaterals it could make voters feel that entry is unnecessary. Conversely, if it goes too far in urging the cause of entry it could encourage opposition both to this and the bilaterals since the latter would seem either ineffective or a commitment to enter which the public is not yet ready to give. Thus while two-thirds of those recently polled were in favour of the bilateral deal, only just over half – not enough to win the necessary double majority – supported either EU entry or the EEA. So, the battle will be a tough one for supporters of integration, because even though there are few supranational implications in the deal, the whole thing can still be seen as an outside imposition on Swiss freedom of action and identity.

However, even if the bilateral package is accepted by the electorate, this will not be the end of redefining Swiss relations with Europe. In the view of many observers, something further is likely to be needed since the bilaterals do not cover all the areas of interest to the Swiss. Indeed they leave some 90 per cent of the Community *acquis* unaccounted for. And Community customs duties and policy practices may still be a barrier. Already, the government has hinted that it will look to other bilateral talks on such technical matters as environmental protection, statistics and the media, but this would not address the main strategic questions of Swiss relations with Europe. In any case, the experience of the first round of bilateral talks is not encouraging. Equally, while as late as 1996 the government was still hinting that the EEA was an option, this no longer seems to be the case. The way the Norwegians have moved beyond this at Amsterdam reinforces this impression.

The government seems clear that only entry will allow them to manage their economic relations and interests successfully. Pressure groups and political parties have, moreover, upped the ante with their demands for entry. Equally, some people think that the Nazi gold affair will push people towards the EU. In fact, for Hans van den Broucke, the bilateral agreement opens the way to a full Swiss 'return to the European family'. Thanks to these and the country's developing membership of the European Conference there could be a new dynamic leading to a reactivated application. However, the EU sees it as very much a matter for the Swiss themselves.

From this point of view it would seem that membership is now the only game in the Alps. Now that the bilaterals have been agreed, the ground has been prepared for entry. On the other hand, the *Alleingang* stance can be seen as reinforced by the way the bilaterals have removed major obstacles to continuing trading with the EU. Hence the SVP has called for the withdrawal of the application for membership since the bilaterals have made this unnecessary. In any case, entry would again raise the trickier political questions excluded from the bilaterals. Dealing with these will be a major element of the forthcoming report on integration. The Integration Bureau is seeking to find out exactly what worries people, but there are still signs that the Federal Council has not fully internalised the constraints that membership can involve. So the relationship between the present deal and entry remains to be resolved.

Simply agreeing the bilateral deal, of course, could not mean immediate entry. There would be a transitional period in which the country remained outside the EU while becoming a more convincing candidate for membership. Optimistic assessments see talks starting in 2000 and entry following in 2004. And the way the agreements worked would be influential in shaping attitudes to negotiation on both sides.

Much will also depend on what happens in the EU. If it experiences difficulties with EMU and its own internal development, this will adversely affect Swiss opinion. Equally, the changes made at Amsterdam, although often derided by federationists, do seem to create more problems for the Swiss, for all that the Treaty seeks to move the EU closer both to people and real subsidiarity. The more cohesive foreign policy, with its defence implications, and its increasing use of qualified majority voting all raise questions about Swiss national self-determination within the EU. Moreover, while the EU is still, in principle, willing to see Switzerland as a member, there remain considerable uncertainties and doubts.

So, while officials and supporters of entry are optimistic, many academic observers, in Switzerland and beyond, are not convinced. They believe that Switzerland will not become a member of the EU in the foreseeable future, thanks to Swiss political culture. Questions of values and identity will be what really count. Until these (or economic circumstances) change, or the coalition of forces favouring integration becomes a real majority, they believe membership cannot be pushed through.

Convincing people that entry will not threaten the Swiss political system, its traditional freedom and its economic prosperity will be hard. This is true even though two-thirds of the elite want Switzerland to join and two-thirds of the population expect Switzerland to be a member by 2010. As previous experience shows, putting too much faith in favourable majorities in opinion polls is unwise. Attitudes change as the actual poll comes closer and both specific policy doubts and the underlying suspicion of the government take hold. In other words there are many obstacles to redefining relations with the EU in the way the government wants and where the logic of events seems to lie.

If Switzerland either rejects the bilaterals or, having ratified them, then fails to secure entry, what are its prospects? Would the country really became an island as some argue? This is clearly an exaggeration. The real uncertainty is what would the defeat of closer relations, particularly entry, do to the internal balance?

In the case of a popular rejection of the bilateral package, two things would seem to follow. Externally, if the deal is rejected then it is clear that relations with the EU are unlikely to grow closer. The view, expressed at the time of the December 1992 defeat that, if the EEA was unacceptable then membership is out of the question, is likely to be reinforced. The Swiss, in any case, would again have to freeze the application, this time for years. Relations with Europe would have to be put on a care and maintenance basis. The Swiss might be able to make some use of the new European Conference and to conclude more cross-border deals. Clearly, though, their ability either to negotiate wider one-off deals or to attract allies would be limited. And it would no longer be the case that Switzerland was the most closely related non-member country.

Internally, the credibility of government and pro-integration forces would be severely undermined. This might not lead to any major political reversal, given the nature of the Swiss system which assumes that governments and others defeated at a *votation* accept their lesson from the people and get on with things. Nonetheless, there has been talk of a change in the *Zauberformel* of permanent coalition at the 1999 general elections. And the government would clearly have no mandate for further approaches to the EU which could encourage the opposition.

The situation would be somewhat less traumatic if the bilaterals were successful at a *votation*, but entry negotiations were consequently either abortive or unacceptable to the voters. If the entry negotiations failed, and some believe that the government would prefer this to a totally humiliating defeat by the people, entry would go off the agenda. However, the government would not lose face, even if isolationist forces would say 'we told you so'. And the country would have to continue with relations based on the bilaterals, albeit perhaps in more expanded form than is presently envisaged. This would also be the case if the electorate rejected entry after the government had negotiated it. However, the government's position, inside and outside the country, would be much weaker. The likelihood of a major change in the internal balance to the benefit of inward-looking forces would be much greater. And, depending on how the Swiss voted, the division between the two language groups could also be exacerbated.

In both situations, of course, this would not be the end of problems with Europe. Commission decisions would continue to have an impact on the country whether they liked it or not. EU policy-making would still constitute a fourth level of governance for Switzerland. This could touch on things outside strictly market-related issues such as Swiss willingness to tolerate political opponents of foreign states. So, politically the country would be marginalised, although opponents of integration would see this as no problem.

Generally, the Swiss would have to do without the kind of access to the market that the bilateral arrangements would provide. Whether this would lead to great economic damage remains a debatable question. If it did, then there is a possibility that attitudes could change fundamentally and create a new coalition for entry. On the other hand, if life continues much as before, the sceptics will have the best of the argument. However, the *Alleingang* school often accepts that inside or outside, structural economic adjustment will have to take place to maintain competitiveness. The effects of this both overall, and on the small business constituency in particular, are unclear. It could also be that further applications would become virtually impossible. Being outside for a continuing length of time would make entry much more difficult at a later date. There would be so much more to absorb and so many more members that the whole equation would be different. EMU would be extremely significant in this context. So the stakes are high, the permutations endless and the outcome highly uncertain.

In a way, this is also true of the country as a whole as it celebrates its 150th anniversary. Redefining relations with Europe is far from the only problem facing the country today. It is much less of a *Sonderfall* than a few years ago. Faced with these problems, arguments about its political system, and unprecedented attacks from America and beyond, it is hardly surprising that Swiss opinion has been described as disorientated.

The underlying problem is that in 1848 the Swiss created a nation state, not the featureless conglomerate sometimes imagined in Britain. And this creation has essentially been defined by its political processes and practices. In the past these have kept the country united and out of trouble. Today, however, they have become problematic. As a result Switzerland is no longer really a model for the New Europe. This is because, at home the post-1848 processes can threaten harmony between the language groups. Abroad, they can compromise the kind of firm and co-operative political line needed in the New Europe. The trouble is that reforming the processes is not just painful in itself but, in the eyes of many, it threatens the essence of the nation. Since change has to be pushed through the existing systems of consensual consultation and direct democracy, opponents of change have, so far, held a veto. It is hardly surprising that the government has yet to find an answer either to the problems of identity or to the existence of an entrenched opposition. They too are the prisoners of their own political culture.

All this shows that, as in the case of Britain, simplistic arguments derived from national character, do not work. Relations with Europe have to be seen as much more complex and institutional. They are also decided by a plural political process. And this is much more than merely a matter of tipping the balance one way or the other. Essentially, domestic politics define the agenda. In the Swiss case they have pushed it to questions of identity. Instrumental approaches to foreign policy do not really cope with this. So the future remains uncertain though, given the Swiss predilection for crabwise progress, it would be an unwise man who prophesied dramatic changes one way or another in the way the Swiss redefine their relations with Europe.

Index